TRADE WITH CUBA: GROWTH AND OPPORTUNITIES

HEARING

BEFORE THE

SUBCOMMITTEE ON TERRORISM, NONPROLIFERATION, AND TRADE

OF THE

COMMITTEE ON FOREIGN AFFAIRS
HOUSE OF REPRESENTATIVES

ONE HUNDRED FOURTEENTH CONGRESS

SECOND SESSION

MARCH 15, 2016

Serial No. 114–150

Printed for the use of the Committee on Foreign Affairs

Available via the World Wide Web: http://www.foreignaffairs.house.gov/ or
http://www.gpo.gov/fdsys/

U.S. GOVERNMENT PUBLISHING OFFICE

99–468PDF   WASHINGTON : 2016

For sale by the Superintendent of Documents, U.S. Government Publishing Office
Internet: bookstore.gpo.gov   Phone: toll free (866) 512–1800; DC area (202) 512–1800
Fax: (202) 512–2104   Mail: Stop IDCC, Washington, DC 20402–0001

COMMITTEE ON FOREIGN AFFAIRS

EDWARD R. ROYCE, California, *Chairman*

CHRISTOPHER H. SMITH, New Jersey
ILEANA ROS-LEHTINEN, Florida
DANA ROHRABACHER, California
STEVE CHABOT, Ohio
JOE WILSON, South Carolina
MICHAEL T. McCAUL, Texas
TED POE, Texas
MATT SALMON, Arizona
DARRELL E. ISSA, California
TOM MARINO, Pennsylvania
JEFF DUNCAN, South Carolina
MO BROOKS, Alabama
PAUL COOK, California
RANDY K. WEBER SR., Texas
SCOTT PERRY, Pennsylvania
RON DeSANTIS, Florida
MARK MEADOWS, North Carolina
TED S. YOHO, Florida
CURT CLAWSON, Florida
SCOTT DesJARLAIS, Tennessee
REID J. RIBBLE, Wisconsin
DAVID A. TROTT, Michigan
LEE M. ZELDIN, New York
DANIEL DONOVAN, New York

ELIOT L. ENGEL, New York
BRAD SHERMAN, California
GREGORY W. MEEKS, New York
ALBIO SIRES, New Jersey
GERALD E. CONNOLLY, Virginia
THEODORE E. DEUTCH, Florida
BRIAN HIGGINS, New York
KAREN BASS, California
WILLIAM KEATING, Massachusetts
DAVID CICILLINE, Rhode Island
ALAN GRAYSON, Florida
AMI BERA, California
ALAN S. LOWENTHAL, California
GRACE MENG, New York
LOIS FRANKEL, Florida
TULSI GABBARD, Hawaii
JOAQUIN CASTRO, Texas
ROBIN L. KELLY, Illinois
BRENDAN F. BOYLE, Pennsylvania

AMY PORTER, *Chief of Staff*   THOMAS SHEEHY, *Staff Director*
JASON STEINBAUM, *Democratic Staff Director*

————

SUBCOMMITTEE ON TERRORISM, NONPROLIFERATION, AND TRADE

TED POE, Texas, *Chairman*

JOE WILSON, South Carolina
DARRELL E. ISSA, California
PAUL COOK, California
SCOTT PERRY, Pennsylvania
REID J. RIBBLE, Wisconsin
LEE M. ZELDIN, New York

WILLIAM KEATING, Massachusetts
BRAD SHERMAN, California
BRIAN HIGGINS, New York
JOAQUIN CASTRO, Texas
ROBIN L. KELLY, Illinois

CONTENTS

Page

WITNESSES

C. Parr Rosson, Ph.D., head of department, Agricultural Economics, Texas
A&M University 5
Mr. Ray Stoesser, president, Texas Rice Council 17
Mr. Jason Marczak, director, Latin American Growth Initiative, Atlantic
Council 36
Mr. Mauricio Claver-Carone, executive director, Cuba Democracy Advocates ... 43
Richard E. Feinberg, Ph.D., professor, School of Global Policy and Strategy,
University of California, San Diego 53

LETTERS, STATEMENTS, ETC., SUBMITTED FOR THE HEARING

C. Parr Rosson, Ph.D.: Prepared statement 7
Mr. Ray Stoesser: Prepared statement 19
Mr. Jason Marczak: Prepared statement 38
Mr. Mauricio Claver-Carone: Prepared statement 46
Richard E. Feinberg, Ph.D.: Prepared statement 56

APPENDIX

Hearing notice 78
Hearing minutes 79
Written responses from Mr. Mauricio Claver-Carone to questions submitted
for the record by the Honorable Edward R. Royce, a Representative in
Congress from the State of California, and chairman, Committee on Foreign
Affairs 80

TRADE WITH CUBA:
GROWTH AND OPPORTUNITIES

TUESDAY, MARCH 15, 2016

House of Representatives,
Subcommittee on Terrorism, Nonproliferation, and Trade,
Committee on Foreign Affairs,
Washington, DC.

The subcommittee met, pursuant to notice, at 1:30 p.m., in room 1334 Longworth House Office Building, Hon. Ted Poe (chairman of the subcommittee) presiding.

Mr. POE. The subcommittee will come to order.

Without objection, all members may have 5 days to submit statements, questions, extraneous materials for the record subject to the length limitation in the rules.

At this time I will make my opening statement. Then I'll recognize members if they wish to make them as well.

In 1962, the United States imposed a trade embargo on Cuba. Fifty-four years later, Cuba is still communist and the Castros are still in charge.

But it has succeeded—this policy—in hurting U.S. agricultural business. In December 2014, the administration announced that the U.S. would take steps to normalize the U.S.-Cuba relationship.

Cuba was removed from the state sponsor of terrorists list. A U.S. Embassy was opened in Havana. The Department of Treasury and Commerce rolled out three rounds of trade reforms. In fact, a new round of travel and trade reforms was announced today.

But it is Congress alone than can lift the embargo on Cuba. This hearing gives us a timely opportunity to examine the changes made so far to the U.S. trade policy toward Cuba and question how the relationship will move forward.

The United States used to be one of Cuba's most important agricultural trading partners. Before the embargo, Cuba bought more than half of the U.S. annual long grain rice. Rice exports to Cuba counted for over one-third of the total U.S. rice exports.

However, this market has disappeared. The U.S. has not exported rice since 2009 because the United States has changed its cash on demand policy. As opposed to paying at the dock, now they have to pay cash before they leave.

Rice farmers were not the only ones hit by the drop of exports to Cuba. Wheat farmers haven't exported to Cuba since 2011.

In 2014, the U.S. share of Cuban market was a measly 16 percent, down from a high of 42 percent in 2009. As I mentioned, one of these reasons was the U.S. Treasury Department's interpretation of the rule that made it more difficult to be a reliable trading partner with Cuba.

The distance between Cuba and the United States is less than 100 miles, as we all know. The distance between the Gulf Coast and Cuba is about 900 miles.

The distance between Vietnam—that also sells rice, also a communist country—to Cuba is 9,000 miles. Exporting to Cuba requires no infrastructure because American exporters have a strong foothold in the Caribbean and Latin American markets but not Cuba.

The Port of Houston would be a natural gateway for trade with Cuba because it already exports a lot of products that Cuba needs. Although some restrictions on trade with Cuba have been eased, there's still a small number of hurdles that put U.S. farmers at a competitive disadvantage.

In Texas, my state, I've seen firsthand how the decline in exports to Cuba have affected American farmers. I'm thankful we have one of those farmers, Ray Stoesser, with us today. He's not a political philosopher. He works the soil and grows rice. Ray, thanks for coming.

U.S. exporters should have an advantage over their foreign competitors because of the lower shipping costs and transit times, and the product is better.

Unlike Cuba's current rice suppliers such as Brazil and the communist country of Vietnam, U.S. farmers can provide year-round availability of high-quality rice that Cuban consumers prefer.

However, the United States is not the only option in town for the Cubans. As the U.S. slowly struggles to sort out what our trade policy is, competitors such as the European Union, China, and other Latin American states are stepping up to get in on the action.

Our competitors don't wait for the United States to make up its mind what it's going to do. It says that the Castro brothers are discriminating against American businesses as a form of leverage. People disagree on that but it could be possible.

We know that the Cuban Government forces American farmers to sell their goods to a state-owned company called ALIMPORT.

Although trade relations have opened up, the Cuban Government has been overly hesitant to actually sign business deals with the United States because our own Government is doing things that are holding U.S. companies back.

For example, U.S. farmers cannot offer terms of credit to Cuban buyers. That means Cuba has to make all the payments up front in cash when purchasing agricultural commodities.

My opinion is the United States Government should revoke this policy and allow the shipper—the agricultural shipper assume the risk in dealing with credit issues with Cuba and not have the U.S. Government prevent the financial transactions from taking place.

In theory, our farmers have the freedom to export to Cuba but in practice the U.S. Government prevents it. It's time maybe to reassume and change the rules to allow our agricultural businesses to assume financial risk.

The U.S. has the potential to be a strong contender in the Cuban market. According to some studies, lifting the embargo could potentially bring as much as $4.3 billion to the United States through exports and may create as many as 6,000 jobs.

I look forward to this hearing and seeing from our witnesses how we can establish a better trade relationship with Cuba that benefits primarily American businesses but also Cuba.

I will now yield to the ranking member from Massachusetts for his opening statement.

Mr. KEATING. Thank you, Chairman Poe, for conducting this afternoon's hearing. I'd like to thank our witnesses. The configuration of this room is such that you seem very far away.

In fact, Cuba is probably closer—but bear with us. We're pleased to have you here and you truly bring some expertise to us.

You're specialists representing the front lines of U.S. exports and trade, academia, advocacy organizations, and I welcome the conversation that we're going to have as the hearing progresses.

The subcommittee previously held a hearing in September 2015 which examined agricultural trade with Cuba with a panel of administration officials.

Since then, the Commerce and State Departments, along with other agencies, have continued toward normalizing relationships with their Cuban counterparts.

In January, the administration announced authorized trade with state-owned companies, which run the majority of the country's commerce, and later this month the President will schedule and make a landmark visit to Cuba, which will be the first visit to Cuba by a sitting U.S. President since 1928.

While this trip will cover many topics, the focus on business opportunities and trade will be front and center. It will be important to hear from our witnesses about their views on the pros and cons of trade reforms that could help U.S. businesses.

I understand the desire for a different relationship with Cuba surrounding new commercial opportunities in the Cuban market.

Currently, Cuba imports about 80 percent of its food, next to the European Union, China and Brazil, the country's two highest suppliers.

There's no denying that there are substantial opportunities for U.S. businesses, particularly in the agricultural industry.

However, I remain cautious with regard to how well-intended policies may impact those hurt most by the regime's policy—the Cuban people.

Opponents claim we have demanded too little from Cuba, particularly in the area of human rights. It should be emphasized that any economic gains made between the United States and Cuba should also accompany gains in civil and the civil society, free media and the ability for political discourse by the Cuban people.

The jury is still out on Cuban Government's efforts to grant additional freedoms. After all, conditions on the island have not changed appreciably.

The Cuban Government continues to jail political dissidents without just cause, engages in other human rights abuses and fails to respect the rule of law.

As we continue to reassess our policy toward Cuba, it's fundamentally important that we strive to strike the right balance between economic prosperity and personal freedoms for both countries.

Thank you, Mr. Chairman. I yield back.

Mr. POE. Chair will recognize members for their opening statements. Without objection, the Chair will recognize Mr. Crawford from Arkansas for a 1-minute opening statement.

Mr. CRAWFORD. Thank you, Mr. Chairman, and I'd like to thank you and the ranking member for holding this important hearing to discuss trade opportunities.

We're currently missing out with Cuba. I also want to thank you, Chairman, for inviting me to be here. I appreciate your indulgence and I appreciate your partnership in efforts to open up the Cuba market for ag exports.

I'd like to encourage my colleagues who favor a more incremental approach to Cuba trade to take a look at legislation that I've introduced—H.R. 3687, the Cuba Ag Exports Act.

This bill simply allows our producers to sell food into the Cuban market just like we're able to do with virtually every other nation in the world.

Yield back.

Mr. POE. Chair recognizes the gentlelady from California, Ms. Bass, for an opening statement.

Ms. BASS. Thank you, Mr. Chair.

First of all, I really appreciate your leadership on this issue and in particular your comments that you made regarding barriers between our two countries.

The U.S. and Cuba have made historic diplomatic progress following President Obama's announcement to begin normalizing relations with Cuba in December 2014.

I note the impressive bilateral steps we have taken regarding law enforcement, counter narcotics, mail claims, travel, commerce, intellectual properties and global health.

While it is necessary to commend the significant steps we have taken, it is also important to note that there is still room for growth in areas of agricultural trade but also in one area I'm particularly interested in and that is health care and what we both have to learn from each other's countries.

And I will mention specifically during the Q and A but there are a couple of areas—one, lung cancer and a vaccine around lung cancer, and another one related to diabetes, and I yield back the balance of my time.

Mr. POE. I thank the gentlelady.

Without objection, all the witnesses' prepared statements will be made part of the record. I ask that each witness keep your presentation to no more than 5 minutes.

As a side note, we will have votes again in approximately 2 hours. We want to finish this hearing before that. I will introduce each witness and then give them time for their opening statements.

Dr. Parr Rosson is a professor at the department head of the Agricultural Economics Department at Texas A&M University. His research interests focus on international trade, international marketing, economic impacts of trade, trade agreements and trade policy.

Mr. Ray Stoesser is the president of the Texas Rice Council and a board member of the U.S. Rice Producers Association. He's a third-generation rice farmer who lives on the family farm in Dayton, Texas.

Mr. Jason Marczak is the director of the Latin American Economic Growth Initiative at the Atlantic Council's Latin American Center. He is at the forefront of the center's analysis on issues such as trade and commerce, U.S.-Cuba relations, China-Latin America energy.

Mr. Mauricio Claver-Carone is the executive director of the Cuba Democracy Advocates in Washington, DC. His nonpartisan organization is dedicated to the promotion of human rights, democracy and the rule of law in Cuba.

Dr. Richard Feinberg is the professor of international political economy at the University of California, San Diego's graduate school of public policy and strategy.

Previously, he served as senior director of the National Security Council's Office of Inter-American Affairs.

Dr. Rosson, we'll start with you. You have 5 minutes. The Aggies go first.

STATEMENT OF C. PARR ROSSON, PH.D., HEAD OF DEPARTMENT, AGRICULTURAL ECONOMICS, TEXAS A&M UNIVERSITY

Mr. ROSSON. Good afternoon, Chairman Poe, Ranking Member Keating and esteemed subcommittee members. I want to thank all of you for the opportunity to testify here today on agricultural trade with Cuba.

I have conducted the economic analysis related to this topic for about 15 years and continue to monitor the conditions there in order to facilitate U.S. agricultural exports and business interests trying to operate in the country.

What we found is that one U.S. job is created for every $76,000 in U.S. exports and furthermore an additional $170,000 in business activity is also created.

Cuba's market for imported foods approaches roughly $2 billion annually. U.S. agricultural exports have averaged about $365 million annually since 2002.

But our exports have been highly erratic. They've ranged from a low of about $141 million in 2002 to a high of just over $700 million in 2008.

More recently, our exports have declined sharply to $149 million in 2015. This product mix of U.S. exports has also changed.

From 2002 through 2012, we exported a wide variety of food and agricultural products—corn, soybeans, rice, wheat, animal feeds, cotton, frozen chicken and turkey, pork, beef, dairy products, dry beans, snack foods, canned fruits and vegetables, grapes, pears, apples, condiments, drinks and treated poles.

So our product mix was very diverse and highly varied during that period. More recently, however, U.S. exports have been concentrated in three primary product areas and that relates to frozen chicken, the soy complex—primarily beans and meal—and finally, corn.

These products together accounted for about 99 percent of our exports in 2015. This change in product mix and the subsequent decline in U.S. exports can be attributed to several factors.

First of all, Cuba has found other suppliers for many of their product needs, particularly rice, wheat, corn and some higher value foods.

We see competition from Brazil, Canada, Argentina, Mexico, Spain and Vietnam, and this competition gains market share at the expense of U.S. exports.

Very often, the competition provides credit and very lenient shipping terms, thereby displacing our products.

Second, our cash in advance payment policy has made our products more expensive to Cuba, leading to delays in shipping and very often costly demurrage charges which are borne by the Cuban Government through ALIMPORT, the food import agency.

Third, a stronger U.S. dollar and subsequently higher priced U.S. products has also had a negative impact on our exports, making them more expensive to Cubans and higher priced compared to the competition.

Fourth, during the global recession, Cuba's earnings from tourism declined along with earnings from other important exports such as nickel. Remittances from Cuban-Americans living in the United States and other countries declined as well, leaving Cuban consumers with less disposable income.

Finally, Cuba is a centrally-planned economy with a portion of food purchases made by ALIMPORT, the central-planned food import agency.

Competitors do not have to go through ALIMPORT to export their products and therefore they are lower cost and more competitive.

Now, despite these constraints, we believe that

Cuba has potential for growth to become a larger market for U.S. exporters. Based on our recent research, we believe that U.S. exports to Cuba have the potential to reach somewhere between $1 billion and $1.2 billion annually and that is because Cuba's demographics are favorable for market growth.

With a population of about 11 million people with a literacy rate of about 99 percent, Cuba has a highly trainable work force of more than 5 million people.

In addition, those aged between 25 and 54 represent 47 percent of the population and therefore in their peak consumption years.

These characteristics are comparable to those of the Dominican Republic, which in 2015 was about a $1.1 billion market for U.S. food and agricultural products.

For this potential to be realized, however, several things are important. The first is impound growth, the second is improvement of infrastructure and logistics and the third is continued growth in tourism and the continued flow of remittances.

Consistent, transparent and facilitative trade policies will also help us stimulate exports as well.

Thank you again for this opportunity to testify. I look forward to your questions.

[The prepared statement of Mr. Rosson follows:]

Testimony of C. Parr Rosson, III, PhD[1]
Before the

United States House of Representatives
Sub-Committee on Terrorism, Non-Proliferation and Trade
Committee on Foreign Affairs

Trade with Cuba: Growth and Opportunities

March 15, 2016

Mr. Chairman and esteemed members of the Committee, thank you for the invitation to testify on agricultural trade with Cuba. I am Parr Rosson, Professor and Department Head in the Agricultural Economics Department at Texas A&M University. I have been at Texas A&M since 1989. From 1997 and until becoming Department Head in 2012, I was the Director of the Center for North American Studies (CNAS) at Texas A&M. I have been involved in research and extension education related to Cuba for 15 years. In that capacity, I conducted dozens of economic impact analyses examining how increasing U.S. food and agricultural exports to Cuba will impact the U.S. economy and the economies of the states that produce those products for export. In 2010, CNAS conducted 18 separate analyses at the request of the House Agriculture Committee examining how the relaxation of travel restrictions and financing regulations would increase U.S. exports, stimulate business activity and expand job growth throughout the U.S. economy. I also testified before the U.S. Senate Committee on Agriculture, Nutrition and Forestry on April 21, 2015. I continue to investigate changes in Cuba and how they affect U.S. agriculture. In general, we find that exports create jobs, and exports to Cuba are no exception. For every $73,600 in U.S. food and agricultural exports to Cuba, one job is created in the United States, along with another $170,000 in economic activity to support those additional exports.

Cuba Market Potential

Cuba's food imports totaled $1.9 billion in 2014 (ONE). Cuba also has the potential to become a major market for U.S. agricultural exports and to develop into a market that is quite diverse, with bulk staple products, such as corn, wheat, soybeans and rice, being important in the near term. But, as Cuba grows and the tastes and preferences of the average Cuban become more sophisticated, U.S. exports will be well positioned to capture a growing share of the high-value food market. Currently, most high-value foods exported to Cuba are consumed in the tourist sector. To put Cuba into perspective, U.S. agricultural exports to Cuba of $149 million in 2015 represented less than one percent of total U.S. agricultural exports of $133 billion (FAS, USDA).

Our previous research indicates that U.S. export potential could exceed the record $709 million set in 2008. With a more open economy, less regulation by both governments, strong tourism and remittances, U.S. food and agricultural exports have the potential to

---

[1] Professor and Department Head, Department of Agricultural Economics, Texas A&M University.

exceed $1.2 billion annually within five years (Rosson, Adcock and Manthei). While much of this additional export volume may be consumed by international visitors, a growing share will also make its way into the Cuban populace, spurring additional demand for food and creating a larger potential market for U.S exports.

In 2015, U.S. exports to Cuba were $149 million, supported $415 million in total business activity and provided employment for 1,555 workers throughout the U.S. economy. U.S. agriculture receives economic gains from increased agricultural exports, with benefits accruing to non-agricultural sectors such as business and financial services, real estate, wholesale and retail trade and health care. Approximately 45 percent of the gains in business activity go to non-agricultural sectors, while the majority of gains, 55 percent, go to agricultural producers, agribusinesses and related firms.

In 2015, U.S. exports were concentrated in poultry, the soybean complex and corn. Major exports included frozen leg quarters and other poultry ($78 million), soybeans and soybean meal ($65 million) and corn ($4.8 million). Together these three product categories represented 99 percent of U.S. agricultural exports to Cuba (Figure 1). Other U.S. exports were feeds/fodders ($9.4 million), dairy products ($1.4 million), pork ($1.3 million) and fresh fruit, prepared and snack foods ($379,000). U.S. poultry claimed 73 percent of the poultry market in Cuba, while the soy complex represented 20 percent and corn one-half of the market. Cuba is now the seventh largest market for U.S. exports in the Caribbean/Central American region, but has potential to become more important.

Cuba is a centrally-planned economy located 90 miles south of Key West, Florida. The proximity to the United States makes Cuba economically, socially and politically important. Since the U.S. embargo was implemented in 1962, effectively severing diplomatic and economic relations, U.S. firms have been prohibited from doing business there.

Nearly three-fourths of the labor force is employed by the government of Cuba (GOC) at a wage of approximately $20/month. The literacy rate is estimated at 99.8 percent, the highest in the Western Hemisphere (CIA). The GOC, however, is involved in virtually every aspect of the business and personal lives of its citizens. Trade and investment are strictly limited and controlled by government regulation. Further, food and agricultural imports are required to enter the country through Empresa Comercializadora de Alimentos (ALIMPORT).

International trade between the United States and Cuba is strictly regulated by both governments. U.S. firms may export foods, agricultural products and medicines to Cuba. Recent regulatory changes allow the importation of selected Cuban products, but these products must be purchased from private businesses, not the Cuban government. So, while some relaxation of regulation has occurred, there are significant regulatory impediments to trade in food and agricultural products.

However, a combination of factors led to the growth of U.S. food and agricultural exports to Cuba during the early 2000s. First, passage of the Trade Sanctions Reform and Export

Enhancement Act of 2000 allowed U.S. firms to legally export their agricultural products to Cuba and travel there for business purposes. Second, the rapid onset of hurricane Michelle in 2001 led to the destruction of most food crops in Cuba, and subsequently to acute food shortages. This prompted Cuba to begin the importation of U.S. food and agricultural products on a commercial basis for the first time since the embargo was imposed.

From modest beginnings of $141 million in 2002, U.S. exports grew to $398 million in 2004 and peaked at $709 million in 2008. U.S. exports then fell to $460 million in 2012, $350 million in 2013, $286 million in 2014 and $149 million in 2015 (Figure 1).

This recent export performance is in sharp contrast to 2009, when a much larger and more diverse mix of U.S. products were exported to Cuba. In 2009, U.S. agricultural exports to Cuba of $529 million required 8,588 jobs and generated $1.6 billion in total economic activity. Major U.S. exports were frozen broilers/turkeys and other poultry ($144 million), soybeans and soybean products ($133 million) corn ($120 million), and wheat ($73 million). These four product categories represented 99 percent of total U.S. agricultural exports to Cuba. Other U.S. exports were dairy products ($412,000), fruit ($228,000), animal feeds ($36,000), dried broths ($32,000) and frozen breads ($18,000).

Figure 1. U.S. Food, Ag & Related Exports to Cuba

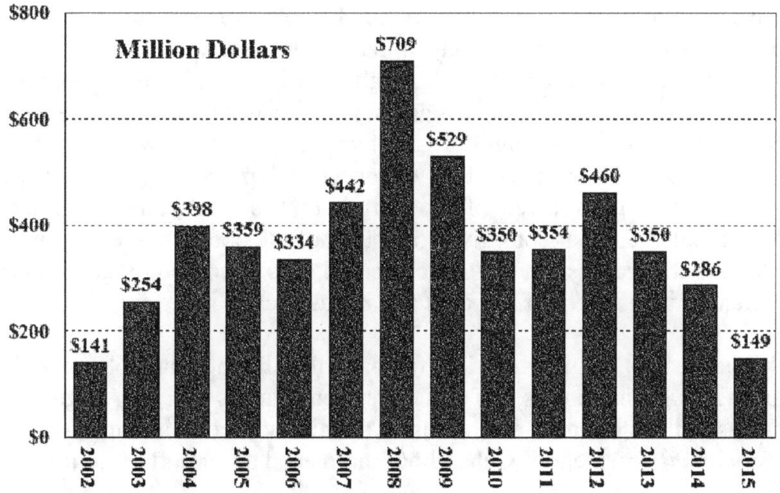

Note: Total exports to Cuba include small amounts of non-ag/related exports.
Source: U.S. Census Bureau, Foreign Trade, U.S. Trade in Goods by Country, www.census.gov/foreign-trade/balance/

There are several reasons for this sharp decline in U.S. exports. First, Cuba has diversified its food suppliers by shifting away from U.S. products in favor of those from Brazil, Canada, Argentina, Mexico, Spain, France, Ukraine, and Vietnam. Credit terms are offered by some of these countries, allowing ALIMPORT to conserve hard currency and use credit to make larger purchases over periods of several months or longer. Sustained high prices for many agricultural commodities and a strong U.S. dollar also negatively impacted U.S. exports over the last several years. Lower earnings from tourism, and nickel exports also hampered the GOC from continuing large cash expenditures on imported food. Perhaps another reason may have been the deliberate decision by the GOC to move away from the United States as a food supplier. After a decade of trying to influence U.S. policy and failing, persistence may have waned. The net result was a loss of U.S. competitiveness and market share, followed by a precipitous 79 percent decline in U.S. exports between 2008 and 2015.

Cuba, however, does have potential for growth as a market for U.S. food and agricultural exports. With a population of 11 million, Cuba is similar in demographic composition and structure to the Dominican Republic, the largest U.S. market in the Caribbean/Central American region, ranging from $1.1 billion to $1.4 billion annually. Cuba also mirrors Guatemala, a market that has grown 38 percent over the past five years.

In 2014, the Dominican Republic had a population of 10 million, with a labor force of 4.9 million. The proportion of the population between the ages of 25-54 was 39 percent. Per capita gross domestic product (GDP) was estimated at $9,200. GDP was composed of 15 percent agricultural production, 22 percent industrial production and 63 percent services (CIA). In 2014, the Dominican Republic imported $1.4 billion from the United States, compared to $1.1 billion in 2010 and 2015, an average annual growth rate of nearly seven percent.

Cuba, by contrast, had a labor force of 5.1 million in 2014 (CIA). Per capita GDP was estimated to be $10,200. This figure includes adjustment for government subsidized food, housing, transportation and medical care. Agriculture accounted for four percent of GDP, while industrial production was 22 percent and services was 74 percent. The proportion of the population between the ages of 25-54 was 47 percent, higher than the Dominican Republic and positive in terms of U.S. export growth potential since that age group tends to experience the highest levels of expenditure on food and other consumer products. These demographic comparisons give some idea of the potential the Cuban food market could have if it becomes more market oriented, less restricted by government regulation and experiences investment in business and infrastructure.

Currently and likely for the near future, three key factors will influence the volume and mix of U.S. food and agricultural exports to Cuba. First, remittances to Cuba, largely from Cuban-Americans in the United States, represent a major source of income and purchasing power for about 60 percent of Cuban households and an important source of foreign exchange for the GOC.

Cuba's merchandise and agricultural exports are also important for sustaining the economy and the ability to import food. With imports representing a much as 80 percent of food consumption in some years, access to foreign exchange is crucial. Tourism ($1.9 billion), nickel/cobalt ($1.0 billion) and pharmaceuticals ($547 million) were Cuba's three most important exports out of a total of $5.3 billion in 2013. Other major exports included sugar ($449 million), tobacco ($245 million) and rum ($154 million). Cuba's ability to purchase food fluctuates widely as global markets for these products influence prices and volumes traded.

Finally, U.S. export success is heavily influenced by decisions on the part of the GOC and ALIMPORT related to which products to purchase, at what price and in what volumes.

The present product mix of frozen leg quarters, soybean meal and corn could certainly increase to include more processed foods and high value products such as pork, beef, prepared meats such as sausage and hot dogs, along with condiments such as sauces, seasonings, mayonnaise, mustard and other condiments. Dairy products, rice and wheat also have strong potential in the market. Snack foods, frozen desserts, soups, gelatins and canned fruit and vegetables all have potential. Raisins, nuts, fresh fruit and vegetables, along with gum, bottled water, wine, beer and spirits all have potential. These products were exported to Cuba to some degree until 2012 when the Cuban government began to make substantial food purchases from other suppliers.

Challenges in the Cuban Market

There are several challenges that limit the performance of U.S. exports to Cuba. Consumer incomes, infrastructure/logistics, and policy and regulation are among the most important constraints. Consumer income growth is one of the critical factors affecting market potential in Cuba. With the large majority of the population on fixed, low incomes, consumer disposable incomes are limited.

Remittances, largely from Cuban-Americans in the United States are an important component of household income and a bright spot in terms of market potential. These funds are transferred directly to Cubans and represent a substantial boost to consumer purchasing power. Estimated to increase eight percent from $2.77 billion in 2013 to $3.0 billion in 2014, remittances are likely to have a substantial positive economic effect on the Cuban economy and U.S. exports, spurring expenditures by those who receive them and fostering additional investment in small business ventures (Cuba Standard). Should remittances decline, however, there would be direct negative impacts on Cuban consumers and followed by lower purchases of U.S. food products.

Tourism is also an important income source for those Cubans who work in restaurants, hotels and other tourist related businesses, such as transportation. With a record 3.0 million visitors in 2014, spending an average of $629/trip, tourism represents a key component of the Cuban economy that generated $1.9 billion last year (Carrillo). Approximately 40 percent of all visitors to Cuba are from Canada, followed by Germany, England, Italy, France and Mexico (ONE). Allowing U.S. visitors to use credit cards will also have a positive economic impact, but the exact amount is uncertain and more research is required.

Cuba also relies on exports of nickel and cobalt, pharmaceuticals, sugar and rum. International market volatility due to wide swings in commodity prices can limit the amount of currency available for food purchases, and certainly dampen U.S. export potential.

Infrastructure and logistics pose special problems for U.S. exporters. Internet access in Cuba is severely limited, with only an estimated five percent of the population having access. While some tourist hotels provide internet access in rooms and terminals in the lobby, many have limited access or none at all. This can hamper U.S. business operations and communications with ALIMPORT officials since some may not have consistent access to email or internet communications. Lack of internet and email can certainly have a negative effect on communications between Cuban officials and U.S. businesses after deals are made and the U.S. representative returns home.

Electrical power, while adequate most of the time, does have limitations. Intermittent outages and complete loss of power are common occurrences. When this occurs, perishable food products located in warehouses, at Cuban Customs, in grocery stores or restaurants may be subject to damage, partial spoilage or complete loss. Additional investment in power infrastructure will be an important factor in determining the amount of U.S. perishables that can be imported and retained in storage. Bulk cargoes, such as corn, soybeans, wheat and rice also face constraints due to antiquated unloading facilities at ports, limited vessel size constraints and slow loading capacities. The development of an efficient, reliable supply chain is crucial to future U.S. export success.

Competition for the Cuban food market is keen. The U.S. share of the Cuban market has been declining for several years and continues to fall in 2016. Many U.S. competitors in the Cuban market offer some form of credit terms to ALIMORT for food purchases. U.S. firms are precluded from doing so and also face an added constraint of being required to offer only cash-in-advance sales, or cash against documents. U.S. exporters cannot use letters of credit to facilitate sales and manage risk, raising the cost of U.S. products and making them less competitive relative to Spain, Italy, some other European Union countries, Canada, Brazil and China (Figure 2).

Reducing the cost and time necessary to process payment for U.S. exports to Cuba would have positive economic impacts in terms of increased exports and economic activity. U.S. exports to Cuba would be expected to rise by $271.2 million/year, requiring an additional $561.9 million in business activity for a total economic impact of $833.1 million and supporting 4,478 new jobs (Rosson, Adcock and Manthei). In summary, consistent, transparent and facilitative policies related to export finance for U.S. exports to Cuba would have positive economic impacts on U.S. exports and the U.S. economy.

Figure 2. Compeition in Cuba Food Market

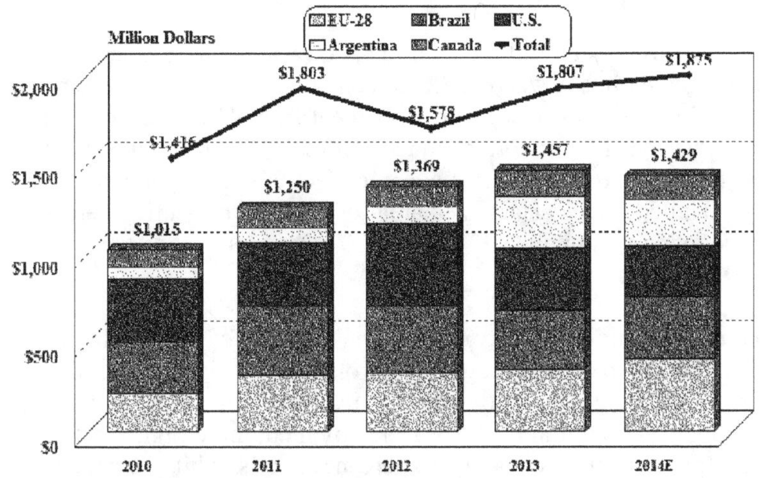

Source: USDA Foreign Agricultural Service; WISERTrade; Brazilian Ministry of
Development, Industry, and Forein Trade; and Argetina Institute of Statistics and Census

Background on Agriculture in Cuba

Agriculture (including sugar) accounts for 4.2 percent of Cuba gross domestic product
(GDP), compared to 18 percent for repairs, 17 percent for public health and
manufacturing at 15 percent (ONE). Cuba has a moderate, subtropical climate with an
average of 330 days of sunshine annually. The island's weather is characterized by a dry
season (November-April) and a rainy season (May-October). The average temperature
ranges from 75 degrees in the West to 80 degrees in the East. Humidity averages about
80 percent and average annual rainfall is 52 inches, with about 39 inches falling during
the rainy season (Cuba Weather).

Roughly 50 percent of Cuba's land is classified as agricultural, with 75 percent of that
land area in relatively flat to gently rolling terrain and suitable for tropical and subtropical
agricultural production (USDA). According to the Food and Agriculture Organization of
the United Nations, however, about 70 percent of Cuba's arable land has low organic
matter content, 45 percent is characterized by low fertility, 42 percent is eroded and 40 is
poorly drained. These soil conditions are attributed to poor land management, including
continuous tillage, overgrazing, and inadequate or improper use of irrigation and drainage
systems.

Agricultural land in Cuba is evenly distributed between cropland (46 percent) and pasture
(54 percent) (USDA). Recently, a large, but so far undocumented, amount of Cuba's
cropland was taken out of permanent crop production and placed in native, unimproved
pasture. It is suspected that this was done in an attempt to increase milk production,
which has declined about 10 percent since 2003. This occurred as milk output per cow

actually increased 25 percent over the same period (ONE). Cereals (rice and corn), sugar cane, tropical fruits, and vegetables accounted for 84 percent of harvested area in 2013.

Cuba's field crop yields, harvested area and production have varied widely over the past decade. Corn yields averaged 47 bushels/acre in 2013, compared to 160 bushels/acre in the United States. These yields, however, were up 20 percent from 41 bushels/acre in the period from 2003-08. Harvested area for corn declined from 556,000 acres in 2010 to 440,000 acres in 2013. In 2013, Cuba rice yields averaged 3,000 pounds per acre, compared to 7,400 in the United States. Harvested area for rice was down five percent to 489,000 acres. Rice production was up in 2013 to 677,000 metric tons, however, nearly 20 percent more than 2010.

Because of poor soil conditions, high humidity, timing and amounts of rainfall, high insect infestation and lack of pesticide or biological controls, Cuba's ability to produce grain and oilseed crops is limited and likely to remain so over the long term. According to FAO, 42 percent of Cuba's agricultural land is affected by medium to highly erodible soils. Poor drainage and low fertility affect 40 to 44 percent of soils, while 70 percent experience low organic matter. As a result, Cuba will remain one of the top grain and oilseed product markets in the Caribbean region.

International Visitors in Cuba

A record 3.0 million international visitors traveled to Cuba in 2014, up from 2.0 million in 2004. Slightly more than 91,000 international visitors were U.S. business representatives and other approved categories. Revenue from international visitors is a major source of foreign exchange for the government of Cuba (GOC), ranked third behind technical services and remittances. It is also an important source of income for Cubans working in tourism such as wait staff, taxi drivers and tour operators. This revenue was equivalent to 57 percent of all merchandise exports in 2009 and 28 percent of the balance of all services trade for 2007. Further, as Cuban tourism earnings increased by six percent from 2006 to 2008, U.S. exports doubled. As earnings from tourism declined 11 percent in 2009, U.S. exports fell by 25 percent. The potential increases in U.S. food and agricultural exports to Cuba due to increased travel range from $48 million to $366 million/year, creating up to 5,500 new jobs, these estimates include only the additional spending by new U.S. visitors to Cuba (Rosson, Adcock and Manthei).

Changes implemented by the GOC in April 2008 allow Cubans to stay at some tourist hotels and resorts (Dominican Today). Many of the 4 and 5 star facilities are out of the price range of most locals who earn the equivalent of about $20/month. During the low season of 2009 (August), however, some of the 2 and 3 star hotels in Varadero, Cuba's major tourist beach resort area, were booking one-week stays to locals for around $200/week (Global Post). With about 60 percent of Cubans having access to hard currency (Calgary Herald) either from remittances, factory and farm bonuses, or tips, these 'new' tourists, are creating some additional demand for U.S. food products.

While many other forces also influenced U.S. exports, and cause-effect may be debatable, there does appear to be a fairly strong linkage between the amount of money Cuba earns from visits to the island and the amount of food it can afford to import from the United States and other suppliers. USDA estimated in 2008 that the proportion of imported foods supplying the tourist trade in Cuba was between 25 and 33 percent. CNAS estimates indicate that the U.S. share of the Cuban food market for international visitors is about 40 percent, implying that each tourism dollar spent in Cuba generates an additional $0.10 to $0.13 in U.S. food exports needed to supply the Cuban tourist trade.

In conclusion, the Cuban market for U.S. food and agricultural exports has potential for growth. From modest beginnings, the market has shown strong growth at times, but also weakness. Our estimates indicate that U.S. food and agricultural exports to Cuba have the potential to exceed $1.0 billion annually, stimulating economic growth as well. These additional exports would support 6,000 new jobs throughout the U.S. economy. For this potential economic impact to be realized, however, several challenges lie ahead. First, sustained income growth and economic prosperity for Cubans is needed. Second, infrastructure improvement and investment will be necessary to improve the efficiency of the existing supply chain and the creation of new cold chains to handle processed foods. Finally, policies and regulations that facilitate trade, and that are transparent and consistent are an absolute necessity. More open trade would certainly lead to economic growth, but absent free trade, the use of financing and letters of credit, improvements in banking efficiency and better infrastructure would stimulate U.S. exports. Thank you again for allowing me to testify on the prospects for U.S. agricultural trade with Cuba.

References

Adcock, Flynn, Luis Ribera and Parr Rosson. *The Potential for Texas Exports to Cuba.* Center for North American Studies Report 2015-2. Available at http://cnas.tamu.edu. November 2015.

Calgary Herald. *Cubans Allowed to Stay at Tourist Hotels.* March 31, 2008. www.canada.com/calgaryherald

Carrillo, Venus. *Tourism in Cuba, So Far So Good*, OnCuba, Fuego Media Group, March 15, 2015.

Central Intelligence Agency of the United States. *World Factbook*, Cuba and the Dominical Republic, March 2016.

Cuba Standard. March 19, 2014. Cubastandard.com.

Dominican Today. *Cubans Can Stay in Hotels.* April 1, 2008. www.dominicantoday. com.

Food and Agriculture Organization of the United Nations. *Land Resources Information Systems in the Caribbean.* 2000.

Foreign Agricultural Service, USDA. Global Agricultural Trading System (GATS), online database. www.fas.usda.gov.

Global Post. *At Cuban Resorts, the of Tourism Apartheid.* August 10, 2009. www.globalpost.com.

Office of Global Analysis, Foreign Agricultural Service, USDA. *Cuba's Food and Agriculture Situation Report*, March 2008.

Oficina Nacional de Estadísticas (ONE). Republic of Cuba, 2008 and 2015 Series.
   Located at www.one.cu.
Rosson, C. Parr, Flynn J. Adcock and Eric Manthei. *Estimated Economic Impacts of the
   Travel Restriction Reform and Export Enhancement Act of 2010* by the Center for
   North American Studies, Texas A&M AgriLife Research, Texas A&M
   University, submitted for the record to the House Committee on Agriculture,
   United States House of Representatives, March 11, 2010.
www.cubaweather.org/cu.

Mr. POE. Mr. Stoesser, you may make your opening statement. Fix your microphone, if you would. Push that button. Thank you.

STATEMENT OF MR. RAY STOESSER, PRESIDENT, TEXAS RICE COUNCIL

Mr. STOESSER. Mr. Chairman and members of the committee, I am Ray Stoesser, a third-generation rice farmer from Dayton, Texas.

I am president of the Texas Rice Council and serve on the board of the U.S. Rice Producers Association. As a first-time witness before the Congress I am honored and humbled to appear here today.

I will summarize my prepared statement, which has been submitted for the record. The Stoesser farm has been in production for over 100 years. I am blessed that my sons, Neal and Grant, have joined me in farming.

Common sense access to the Cuban market will ensure that Neal, Grant and my grandchildren will be able to continue operating our farm into its fifth generation.

After more than 50 years, it is clear that our Cuban policy defies common sense. It punishes U.S. farmers and costs U.S. jobs. Before the embargo, Cuba was our largest rice export market. In 1959, Cuba bought 51 percent of all U.S. rice exports.

The 11 million people in Cuba are among the greatest consumers of rice in the Western Hemisphere. Cubans consume 125 pounds of rice per person per year. This compares to only 27 pounds per person in the United States.

In 2000, Congress opened agriculture sales and Cuba became our fastest growing rice market. There's a chart that says that. In 2004, the Cubans bought $64 million worth of our rice, providing 1,400 U.S. jobs.

In 2005, the Office of Foreign Assets Control restricted payment terms for ag sales to Cuba. As this chart indicates, our rice sales to Cuba plummeted to zero by 2009 and stayed there.

By 2005, the Cubans had purchased a total of more than $1 billion in U.S. ag goods. Cuban buyers paid promptly and most often paid in cash, contrary to what opponents of the trade with Cuba had foretold.

The only disruption of trade was brought about by the U.S. Government, not by Cuban buyers. Cuba can return to a top market of U.S. rice but no buyer can rely on food supplies if the exporting country's government may once again restrict exports without warning.

U.S. agriculture has become a secondary supplier for rice and other farm goods to Cuba. Cuba's need for imported rice is enough to buy more than the entire Texas crop each year. This could generate almost $27,000 annually for every rice farmer in the United States.

As Dr. Rosson explained, rice is just one of the many ag goods that Cuba must import. Based on a review by the International Trade Commission, we estimate that the restrictions on U.S. trade with Cuba cost U.S. farmers, processors and exporters at least $800 million every year. Sadly, our share of the Cuban market continues to fall.

This January, OFAC reversed the 2005 rule on the term cash in advance for commodity sales to Cuba. But our reputation as a reliable supplier cannot be restored until the Cubans are confident that the U.S. Government will not void contracts or restrict trade.

OFAC has relaxed sanctions to allow export financing for goods that support Cuba's agricultural production, processing and distribution. So financing can now be provided to enable Cuba to compete with U.S. farmers but not to sell U.S. food to Cuba.

U.S. law also prohibits the use of credit, credit guarantees and market development and promotion funds to increase sales of our food to Cuba.

We continue to lose market share to competitor countries that are free to use these other tools. Rice farmers urge Congress to return common sense to our Cuba policy.

We strongly support legislation such as H.R. 3238 and H.R. 3687 to correct these discriminatory effects on U.S. farmers. We urge the repeal of the embargo.

Thank you very much.

[The prepared statement of Mr. Stoesser follows:]

Trade with Cuba: Growth and Opportunities

Testimony of Ray Stoesser

On behalf of
US Rice Producers Association
and
Texas Rice Council

Before
The Subcommittee on Terrorism, Nonproliferation, and Trade
Committee on Foreign Affairs
U.S. House of Representatives

March 15, 2016

INTRODUCTION

Good afternoon Chairman Poe and Members of the Committee. I am Ray Stoesser, a rice farmer from Dayton, Texas. I am the current President of the Texas Rice Council, and serve on the Board of Directors of the US Rice Producers Association. As a first time witness before the Congress, I am especially honored and humbled to appear before you today.

Thank you for holding this timely hearing to review the state of U.S. trade with Cuba. It is unfortunate that this once-vibrant market for U.S. agricultural goods continues to be thwarted by U.S. policies.

Congress acted in 2000 to allow the sale of food and agricultural goods to Cuba. Within four short years the Cuban market had regained its place as one of our biggest rice export markets. It wasn't long until our own government once again frustrated America's farmers by implementing policies contrary to Congressional intent. The present Administration has moved to begin to rationalize U.S. exports to Cuba. Ironically, the policy enacted in 2000 to encourage the export of food and feed to Cuba is now more restrictive than the policy being applied to non-food exports. Rice producers and U.S. farmers are being left behind.

Rice producers strongly support Presidential and Congressional efforts to remove statutory and regulatory restrictions on trade with Cuba. After more than 50 years of the United States unilaterally choking off exports and travel to Cuba, one thing is clear: it is a policy that is not only ineffective, but one that punishes U.S. farmers, and costs U.S. jobs in related businesses.

Rice producers support ongoing efforts to end the U.S. embargo against Cuba. In the immediate term, there are two specific actions that we urge Congress to take to address inequities in U.S. policy and allow U.S. farmers to compete with foreign exporters to capitalize on the opportunities and growth in the Cuban market:

1. Allow U.S. food and agriculture exporters to conduct exports to Cuba on normal commercial terms, by repealing the financing restrictions on agricultural sales in the Trade Sanctions Reform and Export Enhancement Act of 2000.

2. Allow U.S. farmers through their trade associations, "cooperators", and exporters to use funds from industry checkoff programs and the several Department of Agriculture market promotion, development, and credit guarantee programs to promote the sale of US agriculture products to Cuba.

Several bills addressing these issues have been introduced and referred to the Committee on Foreign Affairs. We applaud Chairman Poe for cosponsoring two of these bills that would begin to further rationalize agricultural sales to Cuba

(H.R. 3238 and H.R. 3687). Rice producers urge the Committee to consider these bills at your earliest opportunity.

CUBA: AMERICA'S LARGEST NATURAL RICE MARKET

Before the Cuban Revolution, the United States and Cuba were major agricultural trading partners. Our rice exports to Cuba picked up sharply during World War II, when shipments from Cuba's previous top suppliers—Burma and Thailand—were suspended due to the war. From the mid-1940s up until the imposition of the embargo, the United States supplied the bulk of Cuba's rice imports.

In 1951, Cuba was the destination for 252,878 metric tons of U.S. rice, approximately $52 million in sales that represented 51% of U.S. rice exports at that time. Rice exports to Cuba during the period between 1951 and 1960 averaged approximately 169,000 metric tons, valued at $37 million annually and accounting for 25% of all rice exports for the decade.[1] Following the overthrow of the Batista government in 1959, the unilateral U.S. embargo closed the Cuban market in 1960.

In addition to shutting off exports to Cuba, export embargoes imposed unilaterally by our government represent one of the greatest impediments to maintaining and enhancing exports of U.S. rice. For example, the largest market for U.S. rice in the 1950s was Cuba, in the 1970s it was Iran, and in the 1980s it was Iraq. Unfortunately for rice producers and the rice industry, unilateral embargoes imposed by our own government later negatively affected each of these important markets.

Rice farmers have known for decades what the U.S. Department of Agriculture concluded in 1997, that "Of all grains exported by the United States, rice has been particularly hard-hit by trade restrictions."[2] The Department went on to note that such unilateral trade restrictions excluded more than 13 percent of projected global rice import demand as off-limits to U.S. farmers and exporters.

---

[1] A total of 1.7 MMT, based on US Department of Commerce estimates (SEE Attachment A).

[2] **A Review of U.S. Trade Restrictions and Grain Exports**, Foreign Agriculture Service, U.S. Department of Agriculture, http://www.fas.usda.gov/grain/circular/1997/97-09/feature/trd_rstr.htm .

On average, approximately 50 percent of the U.S. rice crop moves into export channels each year. Every level of the U.S. rice industry, from individual farmers, through handlers, dryers, millers, marketers, and exporters are dependent on our export markets for their livelihoods. So having our own government restrict our access to traditionally strong markets for U.S. rice directly affects the ability of U.S. rice farmers to earn a living.

Fortunately, as policymakers have recognized the ineffectiveness of trade embargoes, most of these embargoes have been lifted. Only the embargo against trade with and travel to Cuba remains. Industry, the public, and policy makers alike widely recognize the embargo as having been a failure. The embargo should be ended.

THE 2000 EXPORT ENHANCEMENT ACT REOPENED RICE TRADE WITH CUBA

Congress provided for the resumption of trade with Cuba when it passed the Trade Sanctions Reform and Export Enhancement Act of 2000. The Act sought to achieve its goal of enhancing U.S. agricultural export opportunities by explicitly exempting sales of food and medicine from the exercise of *any* economic embargo. In part this was in recognition of the longstanding U.S. policy not to use food as a weapon in foreign policy.

In deference to Congressional opponents of food sales to Cuba, the 2000 Act prevents the extension of credit in connection with agricultural sales to Cuba by any U.S. entity. Specifically, the Act limits the financing terms of agricultural sales to Cuba to either—

(A) Payment of cash in advance; or
(B) Financing by third country financial institutions (excluding United States persons or Government of Cuba entities), except that such financing may be confirmed or advised by a United States financial institution.

Cuba first made purchases of U.S. agricultural products under the new Export Enhancement Act authorities in December 2001. Between 2001 and early 2005, Cuba contracted to purchase approximately $1.25 billion worth of U.S. agricultural goods. These purchases included shipments of nearly 320,000 tons of U.S. rice, worth a reported $81 million. In 2004 the Cubans bought $64 million worth of U.S. rice – more than their purchases of any other commodity. This established Cuba as our fastest growing market overall, and one of the top five customers for long grain rice.

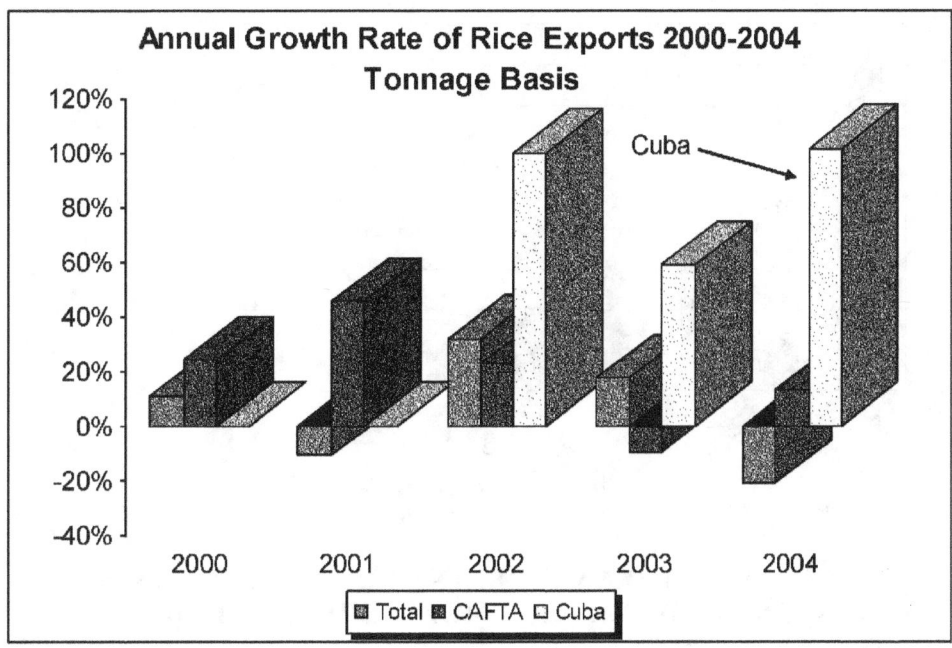

The majority of this trade was conducted on a cash basis, pursuant to licenses issued by the Department of Commerce. Cuban purchasers generally paid promptly, and there was no extension of credit to Cuba by U.S. entities. Clearly, the bipartisan improvements made by Congress in the 2000 Act were working to enhance exports on a cash basis, as Congress had intended. Fears that Cuban purchasers would not pay in full and on time proved to be unfounded.

In 2004 alone, the U.S. exported 177,000 tons of rice to Cuba worth an estimated $64 million with a total economic impact on local U.S. economies of $220 million, and provided for up to 1,400 jobs.

Cuba has the potential to once again become a top export market for U.S. rice, representing a 400,000 to 600,000 metric ton export market under normal commercial trade.

Largest US Milled Rice Export Markets, 2004

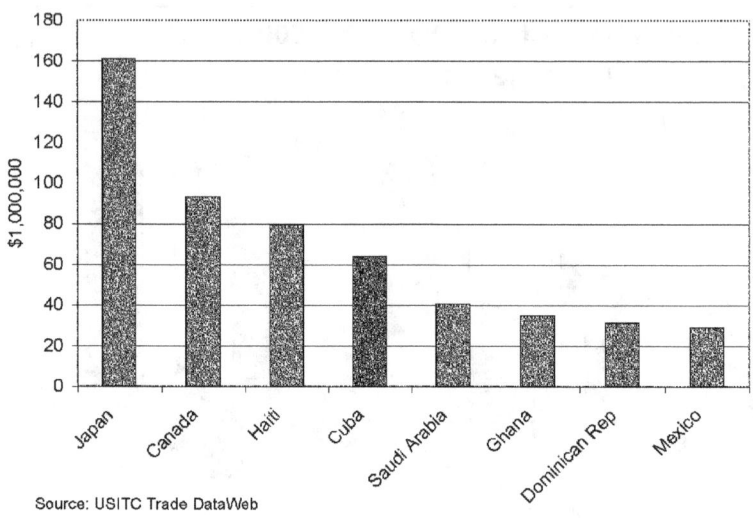

Source: USITC Trade DataWeb

OFAC's 2005 CASH IN ADVANCE "REINTERPRETATION" IMPOSED UNWARRANTED TRADE RESTRICTIONS AND CRIPPLED U.S. EXPORTS

Beginning in November of 2004 the Treasury Department's Office of Foreign Assets Control (OFAC) began holding up payments to U.S. sellers doing business with Cuba, and imposing new regulatory reviews and/or licensing requirements on U.S. sellers and their banks. On February 22, 2005, OFAC issued a Final Rule revising the regulations governing the payment terms permitted for the sale of licensed agricultural products to Cuba (70 Fed. Reg. 9225; the "2005 Rule").

The new trade restrictions in the Final Rule were published without any prior notice to Congress or to the exporting community, nor was any opportunity afforded for comment by the agricultural or exporting communities. The newly restrictive reinterpretation rendered invalid $250 million worth of open agricultural export contracts, and imposed expensive new requirements to finance trades through banks in foreign countries.

Rice producers and the rice industry were particularly disappointed that in imposing this new restriction on exports to Cuba, OFAC ignored the requirement in section 903 of the 2000 Export Enhancement Act that prohibits the President from imposing any new restriction or condition on commercial export sales of agricultural commodities unless the President submits a report to Congress regarding the restriction 60 days before its imposition, _and_ the Congress enacts a joint resolution approving the report.[3]

As we predicted at the time of the imposition of the 2005 Rule, it devastated the market for sales of U.S. rice to Cuba. As the following chart indicates, U.S. rice sales to Cuba plummeted from $64 million in 2004 to ZERO in 2009.

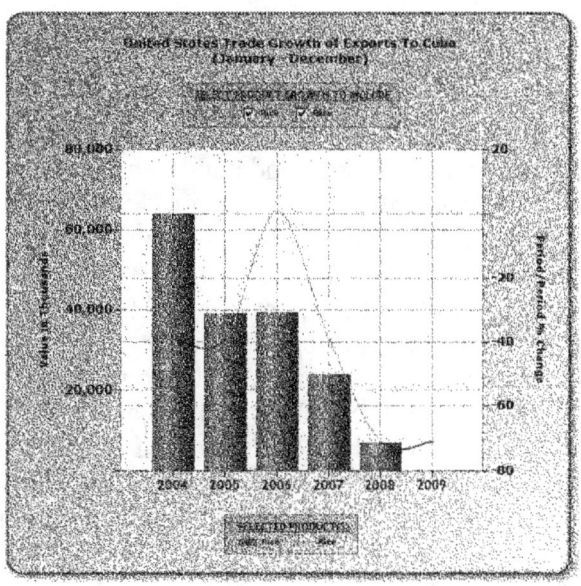

Why did this happen? The Rule and its heavy-handed imposition sent the clear message to Alimport, the Cuban food importing agency, that the United States

---

[3] Section 903(a) of the Export Enhancement Act (22 U.S.C 2207(a)) reads as follows:
"Sec. 903. Restriction.

     "(a) New sanctions. Except as provided in sections 7203 and 7204 of this title and notwithstanding any other provision of law, the President may not impose a unilateral agricultural sanction or unilateral medical sanction against a foreign country or foreign entity, unless –

          "(1) not later than 60 days before the sanction is proposed to be imposed, the President submits a report to Congress that -

               "(A) describes the activity proposed to be prohibited, restricted, or conditioned; and

               "(B) describes the actions by the foreign country or foreign entity that justify the sanction; and

          "(2) there is enacted into law a joint resolution stating the approval of Congress for the report submitted under paragraph (1)."

Section 902(6) and 902(2)(E) of the Act make clear that the prohibited unilateral agricultural sanctions under section 903(a) include "any prohibition, restriction, or condition on carrying out" "any commercial export sale of agricultural commodities".

could not be trusted as a reliable supplier of food and agriculture products to feed the Cuban people. At the time of the Final Rules' imposition, the Cubans had purchased more than $1 billion in U.S. food and farm goods. Despite the dire warnings of those opposed to food exports to Cuba, the Cubans paid cash for all of these deliveries, and had done so in a timely manner. As a reward for building this excellent trade relationship, the U.S. government unilaterally imposed a new interpretation of the "cash in advance" requirement that made illegal the terms of the trade that had been contemplated by Congress and proven by commercial success.

No reasonable buyer can rely on an export seller for critical food supplies knowing that the exporting country's government can (and will) change export policies at a whim. As a result, U.S. agriculture has been relegated to a position as a secondary, residual supplier for rice and many other agricultural goods to Cuba. It is difficult to overstate the importance for U.S. agriculture, its farmers and exporters of maintaining our reputation as a reliable supplier of our exports.

Another result of the 2005 Rule is that it drove most if not all payments for remaining U.S. agricultural sales to Cuba to be conducted via a letter of credit issued by a third country (non-Cuban) bank. This requirement unnecessarily drove up the transaction costs to U.S. sellers and Cuba alike, and reduced the competitiveness of U.S. agricultural products to Cuba. These increased costs and complexities fell disproportionately on small exporters, and were ultimately borne by U.S. farmers. Effectively the Rule enriched foreign banks at the expense of U.S. farmers, processors, and exporters and drove the jobs associated with these activities to overseas competitors.

US POLICY RESTRICTING AGRICULTURAL SALES HAS COST U.S. FARMERS BILLIONS

How much did OFAC's unilateral changes in the terms of these sales cost U.S. agriculture? A precise amount is difficult to pinpoint. But several researchers and agricultural economists agree that the amount is in the billions of dollars. And this is only since OFAC's 2005 Rule disrupted trade.

Cuba's overall agricultural imports grew significantly beginning in 2000. Since 2000, the value of imports more than tripled, increasing from approximately $550 million in 2000 to more than $1.8 billion in 2008. Cuba's imports continue at about $1.8 billion annually. Today Cuba imports close to 80 percent of its food.

The United States, only 90 miles away, is the natural supplier for much of this food.

Unfortunately, U.S. policies continue to discourage Cuba from purchasing agriculture goods from the United States. We continue to lose market share to competitors in other countries that are able to offer financing and do not have the cloud of government intervention overhanging their ability to reliably supply the Cuban market.

In June 2009 the US International Trade Commission published a report estimating the effects of lifting the restrictions on agricultural export financing terms and travel to Cuba, based on 2008 trade statistics. The ITC reported that:

> *In 2008, Cuba imported roughly $1.8 billion in agricultural products, of which $708 million came from the United States. With restrictions lifted, U.S. exports would have been approximately $924 million to $1.2 billion, an increase of $216–478 million. In terms of share, the actual U.S. share was 38 percent. Absent the restrictions, the share would have been 49 64 percent.[4]*

Based on the ITC's conclusions when applied to Cuba's actual imports, we estimate that the losses to U.S. agriculture of our current policies total between $3 billion and $5 billion since 2008. This does not include sales lost between 2005 and 2008.

As a result of U.S. policies, American agribusiness continues to lose ground to countries whose exporters are able to offer financing. Consequently, the U.S. fell from its position as the number on supplier of agricultural products from 2003 to 2012. The U.S. is now Cuba's number four supplier after the European Union, Brazil, and Argentina. While U.S. exports to Cuba have fallen in absolute terms and as a share of the Cuban market over the past ten years, U.S. competitors' share of the Cuban market has increased. The drastic nature of this declining market for U.S. agriculture is reflected starkly in the following graphs.

---

[4] "U.S. Agricultural Sales to Cuba: Certain Economic Effects of U.S. Restrictions", Office of Industries, U.S. International Trade Commission, June 2009, page 8.

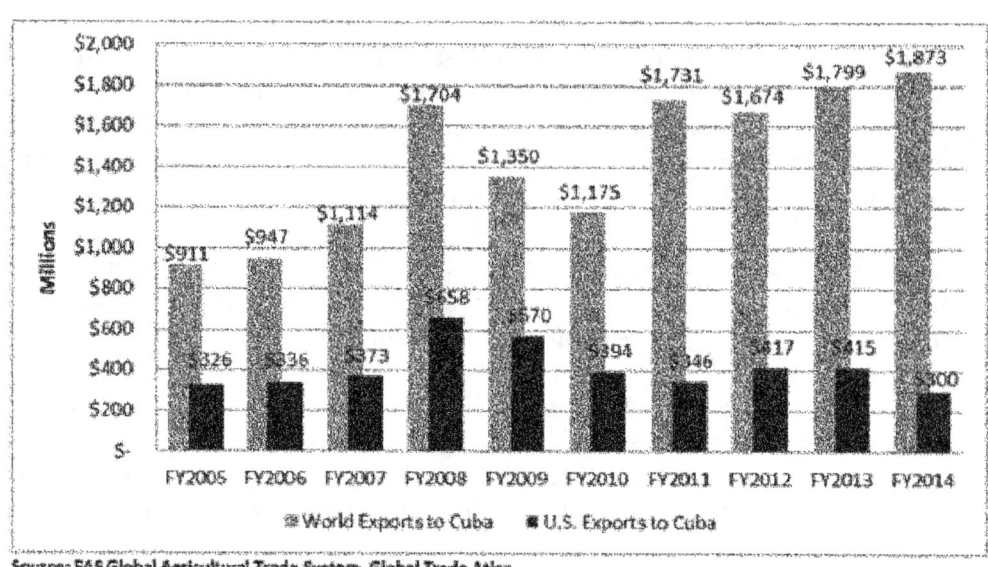

Source: FAS Global Agricultural Trade System, Global Trade Atlas

US Losing Market Share in Cuba

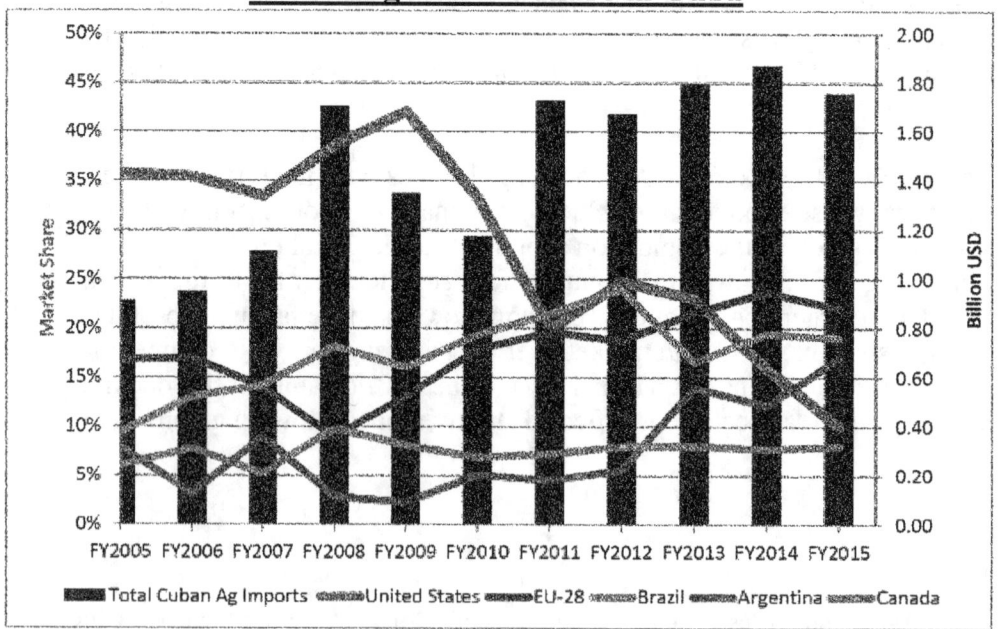

Source: USDA-FAS, Global Agricultural Trade System (GATS)

The story is even starker for U.S. rice exports. As the graph below illustrates, once rice sales began again in 2002, U.S. rice gained consistently in sales to the Cuban market as measured both by quantity and by share of the Cuban market. That progress was abruptly reversed when OFAC published its 2005 Rule, calling into question the ability of U.S. exporters to reliably supply the Cubans with basic food staples. By 2009 U.S. rice exports to Cuba had declined virtually to nothing, where they have remained ever since.

Cuban Rice Imports: Lost U.S. Market Share

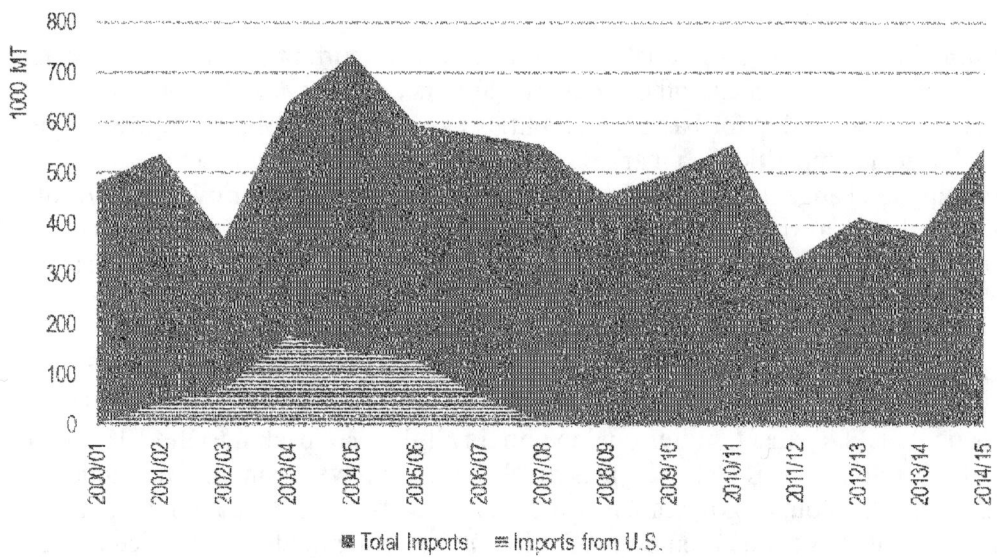

Source: Prepared by Engage Cuba, USACC from USDA FAS data

Ironically, in light of the U.S. government's intervention in the market, the Cubans turned to communist Vietnam to source much of their rice. The quality of Vietnam's rice is widely viewed as being less desirable than that of the United States. Rice from Vietnam takes weeks or months to load and deliver to Cuba, versus only days from the United States. The actions of the U.S. government effectively negated the time, place, and quality advantages of the U.S. industry, particularly for long grain rice produced in the South and shipped from southern ports. Worsening the situation, the Vietnamese could offer their rice on credit as opposed to cash terms.

Since 2009 Cuba continues to import about 400,000 to 600,000 tons of rice annually. At recent prices of $375 to $400 per ton, this equates to $150 to $240 million in rice sales annually, or about $26,667 for each of the 9,000 rice farmers in the United States.

From the perspective of Texas, where production of rice in 2014 was about 500,000 tons, our producers could sell the state's entire annual crop to Cuban buyers if only the restrictions imposed by our own government were removed. You have to believe that that kind of demand increase would make a difference to Texas rice farmers!

From the view of an individual rice producer it is important to remember several things. More than in any other industry, farmers are price-takers, not price-makers. The market for basic commodities like rice are among the few examples of "perfect competition", a market where a single producer can do little or nothing to change the supply, demand, and pricing of his or her own crop, or of the market as a whole. In light of this, every significant market for U.S. rice is important in creating and growing opportunities for U.S. rice producers to sustain their livelihood.

In the case of Cuba U.S. rice farmers have a time, place, and quality advantage that historically has made Cuba a natural trading partner. In fact, investments made by U.S. farmers, millers and exporters all the way back into the 1950s can still bear dividends if Congress acts quickly. By this we mean that individual Cubans in and out of government with whom rice farmers have interacted in recent years have fond memories of enjoying specific brands of U.S. rice in their households long ago. The power of branding and marketing is long-lived. As long as this generation of Cubans lives on, investments that the U.S. rice industry made in Cuba decades ago can still pay dividends. But the clock is running and our policies need to change quickly if this marketing investment is to bear further fruit.

THE REVERSAL OF THE 2005 OFAC RULE DOES NOT GO FAR ENOUGH

On January 26, 2015 OFAC once again amended its regulatory interpretation of ''cash in advance'' from ''cash before shipment'' to ''cash before transfer of title and control'' to allow expanded financing options for authorized exports to Cuba. (80 Fed. Reg. 2292). Rice producers and most of American agriculture is of course supportive of this reversal of the 2005 Rule. Unfortunately, this reinterpretation does not undo the damage that has been done to U.S. agriculture's reputation as a reliable supplier and our unattractive position in the Cuban market.

To add insult to injury, the January 26, 2015 Rule relaxed the current sanctions to allow U.S. financial institutions to finance authorized exports to Cuba of items other than agricultural items or commodities. This is because the statutory prohibition on the financing of agricultural exports in the 2000 Export Enhancement Act remains in effect.

In this regard the 2000 Act, as it addresses agricultural exports, has been stood on its head. What was intended by Congress as a method of providing an exception to the embargo for exports of food has become a greater restriction on food exports than for other goods.

In addition, U.S. financial institutions can finance the export of items to support agricultural production, food processing, wholesale and retail distribution in Cuba. But they cannot finance the export of food products produced in the United States.

U.S. exporters cannot compete with countries able to provide export credits to the Cuban import authorities. U.S. law creates a competitive disadvantage for U.S. exports, prohibiting use of credit facilities, export and technical assistance and market development assistance. Credit is a key component of boosting U.S. export opportunities in other countries.

Current law also prohibits U.S. farmers from using industry generated commodity checkoff funds to promote their products in Cuba, or from using the several Department of Agriculture market promotion, development, and credit guarantee programs to promote the sale of US agriculture products to Cuba.

This stands in stark contrast to our competitor nations exporting to Cuba who use a broad range of incentives to encourage Cuba to buy their goods. From 8,500 miles away, China has emerged as Cuba's largest trading partner. Brazil financed $700 million of the $1 billion expansion project at the Port of Mariel in exchange for Cuba's agreement to spend at least $800 million on Brazilian products and services. The EU Development Fund projects $1 billion of investments into the Caribbean region by 2020, including in Cuba. Venezuela's strategic alliance with

Cuba has resulted in the exchange of Venezuelan oil for Cuban medical services. Argentina's agriculture minister signed a bilateral agreement with Cuba for strategic cooperation over the next five years including technical cooperation on livestock, animal products, and vegetables.

So not only are U.S. farmers singled out among U.S. products in being able to sell only on cash terms, but U.S. policy accommodates the financing of competing Cuban food production. And while competing governments use a broad range of policy tools and financial incentives to build their presence in the Cuban market, U.S. law prohibits our producers from using the U.S. export programs that have proved effective in maintaining and growing markets around the world.

To be clear, we do not oppose the announced liberalizations in U.S. policies on trade with and travel to Cuba. But we do urge you to address these unintended and discriminatory effects on U.S. farmers by enacting legislation to allow the financing of food and agriculture exports, and to support those exports through existing export promotion and development programs.

THE PRESIDENT AND THE CONGRESS SHOULD REASSURE U.S. AGRICULTURE AND OUR CUBAN CUSTOMERS THAT THE UNITED STATES WILL NOT "GO BACKWARDS" ON AGRICULTURAL SALES TO CUBA

The damage done since 2005 to our reputation as a reliable supplier of agriculture and food products to Cuba can be repaired over time. But until the Cubans are convinced that our government will not unilaterally void contracts or otherwise restrict trade, we will continue to be relegated to a residual supplier to the Cuban market.

There is one thing that the Administration and Members of Congress can do immediately to repair U.S. agriculture's reputation as a reliable supplier and to reassure Cuban and other buyers. This would not cost any money, nor does it involve changing the embargo in any way.

To accomplish this, the President and each of you can simply state publicly and repeatedly that the United States Government will not impose new restrictions on sales of food and agriculture products to Cuba. Reassure our own famers and our Cuban customers that progress made in opening and servicing the Cuban market will not be opposed or destroyed by government intervention. Such a statement, and its faithful implementation by the Administration, could go a long way to reassuring U.S. producers and exporters, and our Cuban customers, that the United States government will not prevent U.S. agriculture from reliably supplying the Cuban market.

CONCLUSION: A NO-COST, ONE-WAY TRADE OPPORTUNITY THAT BENEFITS U.S. FARMERS, WORKERS, AND THE PUBLIC

Rice producers and the rice industry have paid a high price for our government's failed policy toward Cuba. First in 1960, and again in 2005, Democratic and Republican Administrations alike have driven exports to one of our largest rice markets from robust levels to literally nothing.

The U.S. rice industry in Texas, on the Mississippi Delta and along the Gulf Coast has a tremendous transportation advantage over our Asian and other competitors in reaching the Cuban rice market. From the 1930's through the 1950's and again between 2001 and 2005, U.S. rice farmers, millers, and exporters had built sales to the Cuban rice market with high-quality rice that Cuban consumers prefer.

Unfortunately, actions by our own government effectively suspended that market. The Cuban demand for food imports is largely being met by a number of U.S. agriculture's key competitors in the global market such as Canada, Brazil, Venezuela, and Vietnam. And this is the result almost entirely of actions by our own government.

U.S. rice farmers have been told that export markets are our markets of the future. In 2010 President Obama in his State of the Union spoke about the need to increase our exports:

> *"We need to export more of our goods. Because the more products we make and sell to other countries, the more jobs we support right here in America. ... We have to seek new markets aggressively, just as our competitors are."*

Rice farmers and the entire rice industry support these goals to increase exports and support U.S. jobs. Unfortunately, with respect to Cuba, our government's policy ignores all of the President's wise advice. U.S. government policy *reduces* U.S. employment by choking off trade with Cuba. That policy continues to *decrease* U.S. exports, and cedes this important market to our global competitors.

Rather than aggressively contending for the Cuban market, our current policy keeps our government on the sidelines, while blocking our own team from taking the field.

When these markets are closed off, everyone in the industry is hurt, and farmers predictably pay the ultimate costs of lost markets from their own pockets. These are unnecessary costs that rice farmers should not be asked to pay.

Rice is the most widely consumed staple crop in the world. Rice farmers are proud that their crops have been used to feed our friends and neighbors around the world—that the food that has been the fruit of their labor has been used to build bridges and not as a weapon of foreign policy.

We are not asking for anything special for rice farmers or U.S. agriculture in the case of Cuba. All we are asking is that the law governing food sales to Cuba be amended to end what has become the discriminatory treatment of U.S. farmers and to allow agricultural export sales to Cuba to be conducted on the same normal commercial and financial terms under which sales are conducted with buyers in virtually every other country on earth.

In addition, we ask that you clarify that any prohibitions on "government assistance" to Cuba do not include the collective use by U.S. farmers through their trade associations, "cooperators", and exporters of funds from industry checkoff programs and the several Department of Agriculture market promotion, development, and credit guarantee programs to promote the sale of US agriculture products to Cuba.

We strongly support the enactment of legislation such as H.R. 3238 and H.R. 3687 to accomplish these goals. In doing so we are in accord with the more than 100 agriculture organizations of the U.S. Agriculture Coalition for Cuba working together to re-establish Cuba as a market for U.S. food and agriculture exports.

Thank you again for your time and attention to this important issue. I look forward to addressing any questions that you may have.

Attachment A
Cuba's Share of Total U.S. Rice Exports, by volume and value, 1951-61[*]

Table 9.   Cuba's share of total U.S. rice exports, by volume and value, 1951-61

Year	U.S. exports		Cuban imports from U.S.		Cuba's share [a]	
	Quant.	Value	Quant.	Value	Quant.	Value
	Metric tn	million $'s	metric tn	million $'s	------------%----------	
1951	493,498	94	252,878	52	51.2	55.3
1952	800,402	157	219,282	50	27.4	31.8
1953	707,332	154	253,786	50	35.9	32.5
1954	568,862	107	162,532	38	28.6	35.5
1955	454,454	81	96,702	21	21.3	25.9
1956	824,010	132	144,826	27	17.6	20.4
1957	740,928	124	187,048	40	25.2	32.3
1958	573,856	97	187,048	40	32.6	41.2
1959	690,080	105	171,612	36	24.9	34.2
1960	893,472	130	15,890	17	1.8	13.1
1961	806,758	106	b	b	b	b

[a] Calculated by the authors.

[b] Minimal amounts before the economic embargo was totally enforced.

Source: U.S. Department of Commerce (various issues).

[*] Alvarez, J. and W. A Messina, Jr., Cuba's Rice Industry: Potential Imports From Florida, International Working Paper 92-27, Food and Resource Economics Department, Institute of Food and Agricultural Sciences, University of Florida, Gainesville. Florida, September 1992. ——————

Mr. Poe. Thank you, Mr. Stoesser.

The Chair will recognize Mr. Marczak for his 5-minute opening statement.

STATEMENT OF MR. JASON MARCZAK, DIRECTOR, LATIN AMERICAN GROWTH INITIATIVE, ATLANTIC COUNCIL

Mr. Marczak. Chairman Poe, Ranking Member Keating and members, thank you very much for the invitation to testify this afternoon on trade with Cuba. It's a great honor to be here.

I'll be summarizing my written testimony and will focus on the geopolitical implications of opening trade as well as how to build our commercial relations.

First, to put this in context, it was only 15 months ago the United States reversed a 54-year policy that sought regime change and isolation but yet had clearly failed.

It is also important to put this moment in context in the hemisphere. The pendulum is swinging away from nationalist regimes, whose claim to power partly rested on an anti-U.S. imperialist message. The Cuba rapprochement is accelerating this trend.

Expanding U.S.-Cuba trade opportunities is a strategic long-term opportunity for the U.S. A stronger commercial relationship will open up opportunities for American businesses, empower the Cuban people and move forward broader U.S. foreign policy priorities.

Political liberties for the Cuban people should continue to be a top priority for U.S. policy. But it's time to help the people of Cuba secure greater economic rights as well, otherwise the Cuban people will continue to face economic challenges that could drive instability and mass migration just off our shores.

It was in a press conference in 1955 when President Eisenhower observed that "trade is the greatest weapon in the hands of the diplomats." Trade can not only raise living standards but is an instrument of peace and a means to spread Western values.

Further, opening trade with Cuba carries ramifications for U.S. relations and strategic priorities in the Western Hemisphere. Venezuela plays an important role in keeping the Cuban economy afloat, giving the autocratic regime in Caracas sway in Havana.

Greater U.S.-Cuba commercial relations will chip away at Venezuelan influence on the island, making it clear to those across the region that not even Cuba recognizes that the future is with Venezuela and its anti-U.S. tirades.

Instead, a deeper trade relationship with Cuba will only further strengthen our allies such as Colombia. A stronger trade relationship and the economic dividends it could pay for both sides may also reduce Cuba's need to lean toward Russia in times of economic uncertainty.

Geopolitics aside, the U.S.-Cuba relationship is changing and the world is taking notice. But without congressional action, just as the U.S. is opening to Cuba, American companies are losing ground to international competitors from the U.K. to Brazil and Spain to Mexico.

And just on Friday, Cuba and the European Union signed an agreement to normalize relations, allowing for closer economic ties.

Losing these opportunities to our European and Latin American allies is frustrating. Losing them to competitors such as China and Russia could be reason for concern.

And although the Cuban GDP is only around $77 billion, it is a market with important potential for U.S. companies in sectors such as agriculture, telecommunications and technology and travel and tourism.

Expansion in trade will also benefit the Cuban people. Greater foreign investment, better access to capital and a more robust private sector will lead to fewer Cubans dependent on the government for jobs, income and resources, freeing them to seek greater rights without the fear of job loss.

Although privately-run businesses are replacing the state sector in certain industries, more than 500,000 worked in the private sector, a 240 percent increase in the last 6 years.

What is the way forward? Regulatory changes have largely exhausted what can be done without Congress with today's executive actions further facilitating commerce and travel.

But relations expand beyond just government actions. In 2015 the Cubans were inundated by an avalanche of business executive delegations. This was a moment of building first contact and of exploring the potential trade opportunities in countless sectors.

But while U.S. companies wanted to move quickly, the Cubans have taken a ''go it slow'' approach. To build trust, U.S. commercial interests should be tied both to what is possible under U.S. regulations but also to Cuba's investment priorities. Projects that do not fit both qualifications will fall on deaf ears.

Now, most of the major obstacles left to achieving normalization remain in the hands of Congress. In addition to lifting travel restrictions, measured steps can be taken to remove codified rules that would have a broad economic effect without political cost.

Though executive action allows financing and credit to be easier for certain industries, agricultural exports are exempt under the Trade Sanctions Reform and Export Enhancement Act of 2000.

Congress is also responsible for allowing American telecommunications infrastructure to be built. Finally, Congress can legislate to remove the barriers to Cuba's entry into the international financial institutions.

Amendments to the Cuban Liberty and Democratic Solidarity Act of 1996 would allow both for Cuba to join institutions like the Inter-American Development Bank as well as for funds from the institution to be spent on loans that assist Cuba.

Technical support from the IDB would inject global standards in financial and economic management while providing critical assistance in transitioning to a single Cuban currency, all issues critical for emboldening the Cuban private sector and enhancing U.S. trade.

Thank you once again for the opportunity to appear before the subcommittee today. I look forward to your questions.

[The prepared statement of Mr. Marczak follows:]

HEARING BEFORE THE U.S. HOUSE OF REPRESENTATIVES

COMMITTEE ON FOREIGN AFFAIRS

SUBCOMMITTEE ON TERRORISM, NON-PROLIFERATION, AND TRADE

"TRADE WITH CUBA: GROWTH AND OPPORTUNITIES"

MARCH 15, 2016

JASON MARCZAK

DIRECTOR, LATIN AMERICA ECONOMIC GROWTH INITIATIVE

ATLANTIC COUNCIL

Chairman Poe, Ranking Member Keating, and Members, thank you for the invitation to testify this afternoon on trade with Cuba. It is an honor to speak on such a timely topic at a critical moment in US-Cuba relations. My testimony will focus on the geopolitical implications of opening trade as well as how to build our commercial relations, including the impediments that currently exist.

Nearly fifteen months ago, the United States reversed a 54-year policy that sought regime change and isolation but yet had clearly failed. Instead, Cuba, a country roughly equal to Ohio in terms of population and size, had cleverly used the United States' anti-Castro policies as a political jujitsu to get broader global support and play an outsized role in global affairs. Havana boasts the greatest number of embassies in the Western Hemisphere other than Washington, DC.

Before discussing trade, it is worth commenting on the geostrategic moment in the hemisphere. The pendulum is swinging away from nationalist regimes (examples include recent votes in Venezuela, Argentina and Bolivia) whose claim to power partly rested on an anti-US imperialist message. The Cuba rapprochement is accelerating the pendulum's movement.

Expanding US-Cuba trade opportunities is a strategic, long-term opportunity for the United States. Much has been done since December 2014, but Congress has the power to enact sweeping changes. A stronger commercial relationship will open up opportunities for American businesses, empower the Cuban people, and move forward broader US foreign policy priorities.

Political liberties for the Cuban people should continue to be top priority for US policy. But after over five decades, it is time to help the people of Cuba secure greater economic rights. Otherwise, the Cuban people will continue to face economic challenges that could drive instability and mass migration just off our shores—creating a potential national security threat for the United States.

Opening Trade: The Broader Geopolitical Implications

During a press conference in 1955, President Eisenhower observed that "trade is the greatest weapon in the hands of the diplomat." Trade can not only raise living standards, but is an instrument of peace, and a means to spread Western values.

The economic and the strategic importance of trade cannot be underestimated, and this is particularly true for a country just 90 miles off the US coast. Cuba carries a disproportionate amount of influence around the world and in the region for its size. For example, it is currently hosting peace talks between the administration of Colombian President Juan Manuel Santos and the FARC guerrillas to end one of the world's longest-running armed conflicts. As history has demonstrated, Cuba's outsized global role carries geopolitical implications for the United States. Expanded trade will only enhance ties, allowing for deeper engagement in a number of issues.

Further opening trade with Cuba carries ramifications for US relations and strategic priorities in the Western Hemisphere. Venezuela plays an important role in keeping the economy afloat, giving the autocratic regime in Caracas sway in Havana. Greater US-Cuba commercial relations will chip away at Venezuelan influence on the island, making it clear to those across the region that not even Cuba recognizes that the future is with Venezuela and its anti-US tirades. A deeper trade relationship with Cuba will only further strengthen our allies, such as Colombia, and convince doubters that the United States stands ready to be a partner.

The Cubans are slowly warming to greater engagement with the United States, with the mid-April Communist Party Congress to be a key indication of the extent to which linkages may deepen. But it is no coincidence that as Venezuela faces an economic crisis—including over 700 percent projected inflation this year— Cuba is exploring other options.

Cuba imports more than 50 percent of its oil. Economic decisions are linked to the price of oil, and the fate of its oil-exporting allies. For fifteen years, Venezuela has provided petroleum products to Cuba on preferential terms. Cuba receives more than 100,000 barrels of oil per day in exchange for Cuban professionals, including some 30,000 doctors and nurses, and it provides intelligence capacities to the Venezuelan government. The Cuban government also receives hard currency for its professionals abroad. This arrangement may be nearing its end, opening the door for the United States to come in and play a key role in helping to build the nascent Cuban private sector.

A stronger trade relationship—and the economic dividends it could pay for both sides—may also reduce Cuba's need to lean toward Russia in times of economic uncertainty. This could potentially deny Russia a reliable friend that carries diplomatic muscle in the Global South. On Russian President Vladimir Putin's July 2014 trip to Cuba, he agreed to write off 90 percent, or almost $32 billion, of Cuba's Soviet-era debt. Just two month earlier, Cuba was one of 11 countries in the United Nations General Assembly to reject a US-backed resolution declaring Crimea's referendum to secede from Ukraine invalid.

Pick Up the Trade Pace

Since the December 2014 shift in policy and the three following rounds of executive actions, the writing is clearly on the wall to the world. We are on an irreversible path of engagement. But, still, the United States continues to miss out. Without congressional action, the regulatory changes—while critical to pushing the door open to greater commercial engagement—have yet to produce a substantial increase in US investment and trade deals signed. Of course, the onus is also on the Cuban government and its reluctance to quickly approve projects.

The result: steady reports of new foreign business deals, while the majority of US companies await that first deal. A foreign investment law passed in 2014 helped to accelerate rapid trade growth, which doubled in the past decade. Now, with the alleviation of certain US trade restrictions, it is even easier for other foreign companies—from Mexico, Europe, and Brazil—to do business in Cuba.

Just as the United States is opening to Cuba, American companies are losing ground to international competitors. The Dutch-British consumer products company Unilever, for example, plans to invest $35 million in the Mariel Special Development Zone. The Brazilian joint venture cigarette company, Brascuba, plans to build a $120 million facility in Mariel. Spain's Meliá Hotels International plans to expand from 13,000 to 15,000 rooms by 2018, while Grupo Tradeco, a Mexican construction firm, is eyeing Cuba's infrastructure needs. And just on Friday, Cuba and the European Union (which already accounts for 20 percent of the island's trade) signed an agreement to normalize relations, allowing for closer economic ties.

Losing these opportunities to our European and Latin American allies is frustrating; losing them to competitors such as Russia and China could be reason for concern. Both countries have forgiven debt and made major investments in Cuba in the last year, clearly looking to strengthen their relationships with a country just off the coast of Florida.

More trade with the United States also could provide the Cuban people with critical resources in agriculture, medical supplies, building materials, and telecommunications devices. Though access to these goods has been expanded, Cubans will not fully benefit until the remaining restrictions—particularly those on lending and credit—are lifted. And although the Cuban GDP is only around $77 billion—on par with Hawaii or the Salt Lake City metropolitan area—it is a market with important potential for US companies in sectors such as agriculture, telecommunications and technology, and travel and tourism.

Expansion of trade would benefit the Cuban people. Greater foreign investment, better access to capital, and a more robust private sector would lead to fewer Cubans dependent on the government for jobs, income, and resources. Already privately-run businesses are replacing the state-sector in certain industries. More than 500,000 Cubans work in the private sector—a 240 percent increase in six years, representing 25 percent of the labor force. More trade would significantly boost the number of private-sector workers, creating a robust new class of empowered Cubans who could seek greater rights without the fear of job loss.

Greater economic autonomy for Cubans should be a central goal for US foreign policy as it will create a more independent populace. Throughout the world, and most especially in Latin America, the demands of a strong middle class have forced governments to offer better services and expanded freedoms to their people. Cuba will not be an exception.

The Way Forward: Building Relations

Regulatory changes, including the round in January 2016, have largely exhausted what can be done without Congress. But the administration can still use executive authority to enhance the island's commercial environment and to further US-Cuba trade for the betterment of the Cuban people.

In addition to clarifying the parameters of US financial institutions' engagement and expanding travel to include a general license for individual people-to-people exchange, the administration should remove barriers to the Inter-American Development Bank (IDB) providing assistance to Cuba. There are various avenues to do this, including US abstention at an eventual IDB board of directors vote on whether to include Cuba, or by declaring IDB cooperation with Cuba to be in US national interest. IDB membership would give Cuba access to technical resources critical to dealing with pending financial issues—such as currency unification—along with expertise in managing the new investments coming into the island.

But relations expand beyond just government actions. In 2015, the Cubans were inundated by an avalanche of business executives from multiple sectors, all traveling to learn more about opportunities in a previously closed-off nation and to meet with the relevant ministries. US governors and mayors also traveled to the island. This was a moment of building first contact and of exploring the potential trade opportunities in countless sectors—many of which were interested due to the sheer romanticism of investing in Cuba. But while US companies wanted to move quickly, the Cubans—at times apprehensive given a US policy of regime change—have taken a go-it-slow approach.

To build trust, US commercial interests should be tied both to what is possible under US regulations but also to Cuba's investment priorities. Projects that do not fit both qualifications will fall on deaf ears. Here, it is critical to understand the rationale and thinking of how Cuba perceives potential investments and how well it fits into the 326 projects identified as foreign investment opportunities by the Cuban government. Beyond that, given the over five decades of mistrust, a strong commercial relationship must come with a broader commitment to the Cuban people. Businesses like Airbnb and Sprint have followed this approach and are now operating in Cuba.

The Role of Congress

Most of the major obstacles left to achieving normalization remain in the hands of Congress. The eventual goal should be the wholesale lifting of sanctions. Although this is unlikely in the near term, growing support exists for removing travel restrictions. The administration may further ease travel restrictions prior to the President's trip to Cuba next week, but only Congress can completely remove them. Without travel limitations, US business executives—and tourists alike—could freely go to Cuba to explore new trade and investment relationships with the independent Cuban private sector, unhindered by congressionally mandated burdens on the composition of their trip.

Beyond travel, measured steps can be taken to remove codified rules that would have a broad effect without political cost. Though executive action allows financing and credit to be easier for certain industries, agriculture exports are exempt. The Trade Sanctions Reform and Export Enhancement Act of 2000 (TSRA) prohibits American creditors from extending credit to Cuba's agricultural importers. It will take an act of Congress to overturn this. Since enactment of that law, the United States has fallen from Cuba's number one supplier of agricultural products to number four. Striking just a few lines in TSRA would yield an immediate uptick for US exporters while providing important basic goods to the Cuban people.

Congress is also responsible for allowing American telecommunications infrastructure to be built. Though executive action has permitted the sale of devices and partnerships with Cuban enterprises, American telecommunications companies are still restricted in their ability to construct the infrastructure necessary for a robust system in Cuba.

Finally, although receiving less attention than actions related to travel, agriculture, or telecommunications, Congress can legislatively remove the barriers to Cuba's entry into the international financial institutions. Executive action can get around some of these obstacles, but amendments to the Cuban Liberty and Democratic Solidarity Act of 1996 (known as the Helms-Burton Act) would allow both for Cuba to join institutions like the Inter-American Development Bank as well as for funds from the institution to be spent on loans that assist Cuba. Technical support from the IDB would inject global standards in financial and economic management while providing critical assistance in transitioning to a single Cuban currency—all issues critical for enhancing US trade with Cuba.

In closing, I'd like to quote former US Secretary of Commerce Carlos Gutierrez: "What a lot of people miss who are using the argument that we should not engage economically until there are changes politically, what they miss is that the right to private property, the right to earn a living on your own, and provide for your family is one of our most precious of human rights."

Thank you, once again, for the opportunity to appear before the Subcommittee today. I look forward to answering your questions.

###

Mr. POE. I thank the gentleman.

The Chair now recognizes Mr. Claver-Carone.

STATEMENT OF MR. MAURICIO CLAVER–CARONE, EXECUTIVE DIRECTOR, CUBA DEMOCRACY ADVOCATES

Mr. CLAVER-CARONE. Thank you, Mr. Chairman, Ranking Member, members of the committee. It's really a privilege to be here and join you today to discuss these important and consequential issues surrounding U.S. trade policy toward Cuba.

And I particularly appreciate being given the opportunity to be the sole dissenting voice in this panel, as free expression is a right enjoyed by 34 out of 35 nations in this hemisphere with one exception—Cuba.

So as you are aware, pursuant to the Trade Sanctions Reform and Export Enhancement Act of 2000, the sale of ag commodities, medicine, medical devices to the Castro regime in Cuba was authorized by Congress with one important caveat—these sales must be for cash in advance.

Prior to that, the export of food, medicine and medical devices to the Cuban people, I would highlight, had been authorized under the Cuban Democracy Act of 1992.

I, for one, have no problem with taking cash away from the Castro regime, and that's not a point of contention in this hearing in any way. It's the consequences of expanding these cash sales to bilateral trade, financing and investment—in other words, flushing—giving the Castro regime cash. That should be a concern to us all.

I'd also—I can't help but note that, you know, whatever rice sales had been lost to the Cuban people in 1959 I'm sure has been made up in multiples to the Cuban people in Miami since 1959 since those people are now in Miami as opposed to Cuba.

For years we've heard of how an improvement in U.S.-Cuba relations and easing of sanctions and increased travel to the island would benefit U.S. farmers.

Well, the fact is since December 17th, 2014 the Obama administration has engaged the Castro regime and has provided a litany of unilateral policy concessions.

We've seen the payment terms for agricultural sales have been eased, American travel to Cuba increased by over 50 percent, Cuba's GDP grew by over 4 percent, diplomatic relations were established and all these trade delegations have visited Havana.

So surely, based on this, ag sales to Cuba would have grown exponentially, right?

Wrong. U.S. ag exports to Cuba plummeted in 2015 by nearly 40 percent and that's not the only counterproductive result from President Obama's policy of unilaterally easing sanctions in December 2014. Additionally, we've seen political arrests have intensified.

A new Cuban migration crisis is unfolding. The number of self-employed workers in Cuba has decreased. Internet connectivity ranking has dropped. Religious freedom violations have increased tenfold. Castro reneged on the release of political prisoners and visits by international monitors.

So you may ask what do all of these facts regarding political, civil and economic rights have to do with trade with Cuba. The answer is everything, because the Castro regime is the only client business partner for foreign companies in Cuba.

If we're going to have an honest debate about trade and tourism sanctions on Cuba, it's important to understand how that regime conducts business.

First and foremost, from an economic perspective the very concept of trade and investment in Cuba is grounded in the misconception about how business takes place on the island.

In most of the world, that means dealing with privately-owned or operated corporations. That's not the case in Cuba. In Cuba, the trade and investment is the exclusive domain of the state. There are no exceptions, and that state's exclusivity to trade and investment was enshrined in Article 18 of Castro's 1976 constitution.

That exclusivity has extended to TSREEA sales and we've seen that of the $5 billion in U.S. ag and medical products that have been sold to Cuba, the unpleasant fact is that all of those sales by over 250 U.S. entities have only had one Cuban buyer—every penny—the Castro government.

So we already know what lifting sanctions toward Cuba would look like. TSREEA sales have actually provided essentially the model for this.

It would be Americans in the system whereby commerce is simply a tool to benefit and strengthen Cuba's totalitarian regime and let's remember what we're talking about here. The dominant force in Cuba's economy is the armed forces holding company known as GAESA.

These are the same Cuban armed forces that held a stolen U.S. Hellfire missile for nearly 2 years that were caught twice smuggling heavy weaponry including the worst sanctions violation ever to North Korea, that oversee the most egregious abuses of human rights in the hemisphere, that have subverted human rights and democracy in Venezuela, export surveillance systems technology to other countries in the region, that welcome Russian military intelligence ships that dock in their ports, that share intelligence with the world's anti-American regimes, that have three senior Cuban military officers indicted in the United States for the murder of Americans.

These aren't nice people in that regards. An important issue that I think it's important also here to recognize is that we need to make sure to protect American victims of stolen property.

According to the American Law Review, the Castro regime's confiscation of U.S. assets was the largest uncompensated taking of American property by a foreign government in history.

We need to make sure, and I urge Congress, for example, to pass legislation. If we're going to consider expanding trade and other issues with Cuba, we should consider taking away the President's waiver authority over Title III of the Libertad Act and allow Americans legal standing to pursue justice in courts.

I also think it's very important that we need to uphold U.S. law and international labor norms. Some of the measures that have been recently announced have been in direct—by the Obama administration have been in direct contravention of the letter, spirit and intent of current U.S. law regardless of your position.

Those should be upheld. Moreover, those deals have violated a myriad of international labor covenants including freedom of association, protection of wages, right to organize, discrimination, employment policy convention, et cetera.

To conclude, there are many theories and estimates about how much more money one sector or another can make from conducting business if sanctions were eased or lifted and we're hearing many of those theories and estimates today.

However, as we've learned from the drastic sale over the last year, that's hardly guaranteed and we need to make sure that those are weighed by serious factual considerations regarding the structure of Cuba's business entities run by the military, its beneficiaries, the Castro family and its cronies, the rights of its victims both Cubans and Americans and whether such practices are in our national interests.

Thank you.

[The prepared statement of Mr. Claver-Carone follows:]

Mauricio Claver-Carone
Executive Director, Cuba Democracy Advocates
House Committee on Foreign Affairs
March 15, 2016
"Trade With Cuba: Growth and Opportunities"

Thank you, Mr. Chairman, Ranking Member and Members of the Committee.

It's truly a privilege to join you here today to discuss important and consequential issues surrounding U.S. trade policy towards Cuba. I particularly appreciate being given the opportunity to be the sole dissenting voice in this panel, as free expression is a right enjoyed by 34-of-35 nations in this Western Hemisphere, with only one exception – Cuba.

My name is Mauricio Claver-Carone and I'm the Executive Director of Cuba Democracy Advocates, a non-profit, non-partisan organization dedicated to the promotion of human rights, democracy and the rule of law in Cuba.

Obama's Policy Changes Have Proven Counter-Productive

As you are aware, pursuant to the Trade Sanctions Reform and Export Enhancement Act of 2000 ('TSREEA'), the sale of agricultural commodities, medicine and medical devices to the *Castro regime* in Cuba was authorized by Congress, with one important caveat – these sales must be for cash-in-advance. Prior to that, the export of food, medicine and medical devices to the *Cuban people* had been authorized under the Cuban Democracy Act of 1992 ('CDA'). I, for one, have no problem with taking cash *away* from the Castro regime. That is not a point of contention in this hearing. It's the consequences of expanding cash-in-advance sales to bilateral trade, financing and investment – in other words, *flushing* the Castro regime with cash – that should concern us all.

For years we've heard how an improvement in U.S.-Cuba relations, an easing of sanctions and an increase in travel to the island, would benefit U.S. farmers. Well, since December 17th, 2014, the Obama Administration has engaged the Castro regime and has provided a litany of unilateral policy concessions.

As part of these concessions, the Obama Administration eased payment terms for agricultural sales; American travel to Cuba increased by over 50%; Cuba's GDP grew by over 4%; diplomatic relations were established; and endless U.S. business and trade delegations have visited Havana.

Thus, surely U.S. agricultural sales to Cuba would have grown exponentially, right? *Wrong*.

U.S. agricultural exports to Cuba *plummeted* by nearly 40% in 2015. In August alone, the value of U.S. agricultural exports dropped 84% to $2.25 million from $14.30 million in 2014. That's one of the lowest numbers since the United States authorized agricultural exports to the Castro regime in 2000.

And that's not the only counter-productive result of President Obama's policy of unilateral easing sanctions in December 2014. Additionally:

- **Political arrests have intensified.** Throughout 2015, there were more than 8,616 documented political arrests in Cuba. In November alone there were more than 1,447 documented political arrests, the highest monthly tally in decades. Those numbers compare to 2,074 arrests in 2010 and 4,123 in 2011.

- **A new Cuban migration crisis is unfolding.** The United States is faced with the largest migration of Cuban immigrants since the rafters of 1994. The number of Cubans entering the United States in 2015 was nearly *twice* that of 2014. Some 51,000 Cubans last year entered the United States; tens of thousands more are desperately trying to make the journey, via Ecuador and other South and Central American countries. When President Obama took office, the numbers were less than 7,000 annually.

- **The number of "self-employed" workers in Cuba has decreased.** The Cuban government today is licensing 10,000 fewer "self-employed" workers than it did in 2014. In contrast, Castro's military monopolies are expanding at record pace. The Cuban military-owned tourism company, Gaviota S.A., announced 12% growth in 2015 and expects to double its hotel business this year. Even the limited spaces in which "self-employed" workers previously operated are being squeezed as the Cuban military expands its control of the island's travel, retail and financial sectors of the economy.

- **Internet "connectivity ranking" has dropped.** The International Telecommunication Union's (ITU) Measuring the Information Society Report for 2015, the world's most reliable source of data and analysis on global access to information and communication. ITU has dropped Cuba's ranking to 129 from 119. The island fares much worse than some of the world's most infamous suppressors of the Internet suppressors, including Zimbabwe (127), Syria (117), Iran (91), China (82) and Venezuela (72).

- **Religious freedom violations have increased tenfold.** According to the London-based NGO, Christian Solidarity Worldwide ('CSW'), last year 2,000 churches were declared illegal and 100 were designated for demolition by the Castro regime. Altogether, CSW documented 2,300 separate violations of religious freedom in 2015 compared to 220 in 2014.

- **Castro reneged on the release of political prisoners and visits by international monitors.** Most of the 53 political prisoners released in the months prior and after Obama's December 2014 announcement have since been re-arrested on multiple occasions. Five have been handed new long-term prison sentences. Meanwhile, Human Rights Watch noted in its new 2016 report, "*Cuba has yet to allow visits to the island by the International Committee of the Red Cross or by U.N. human rights monitors, as stipulated in the December 2014 agreement with the United States.*"

You may ask – what do these facts and figures on political, civil and economic rights have to do with trade with Cuba? The answer is: *Everything* -- because the Castro regime is the only client/business partner for foreign companies in Cuba.

The Reality of Doing Business in Cuba

In order to have an honest debate about trade and tourism sanctions on Cuba, it's important to understand how that totalitarian regime conducts business.

First and foremost, from an economic perspective, the very concept of trade and investment in Cuba is grounded in a misconception about how "business" takes place on the island. In most of the world, trade and investment means dealing with privately-owned or operated corporations. That's not the case in Cuba. In Cuba, foreign trade and investment is the exclusive domain of the state, i.e. Fidel and Raul Castro. There are no "exceptions."

Here's a notable fact: In the last five decades, *every* single "foreign trade" transaction with Cuba has been with a state entity, or individual acting on behalf of the state. The state's exclusivity regarding trade and investment was enshrined in Article 18 of Castro's 1976 Constitution.

The state's exclusivity extends also to what the rest of the world considers to be "humanitarian" transactions. Since the passage of TSREEA in 2000, nearly $5 billion in U.S. agricultural and medical products have been sold to Cuba. It is an unpleasant fact, however, that all those sales by more than 250 privately-owned U.S. companies were made to *only one* Cuban buyer, the Castro government.

As the U.S. Department of Agriculture's own report on Cuba notes, "*The key difference in exporting to Cuba, compared to other countries in the region, is that all U.S. agricultural exports must be channeled through one Cuban government agency, ALIMPORT.*"

Therefore, it should be no surprise then that these U.S. products end up with huge price mark-ups, on the shelves of the stores set up by the Castro regime that only accept "hard currencies," such as the U.S. dollar or Euro. These are stores where mostly tourists shop. Little of the food or medicine is made available to Cuba's general population.

This being the case with the sale of U.S. food and medicine, try imagining the disproportionate benefit the Cuban regime has derived from three decades of unfettered trade with the Soviet bloc, or the billions in European and Canadian trade and investment in the Cuban state since the collapse of the Soviet Union in 1991. There is not a shred of evidence to suggest any of the benefits got beyond the Castro regime.

Hence we already know what lifting sanctions towards Cuba would look like. TSREEA sales from the U.S. and business ventures with other nations exhibit the

model: A mercantilist system whereby commerce is simply a tool to benefit and strengthen Cuba's totalitarian regime.

The dominant force in Cuba's economy is the armed forces' holding company, called GAESA. Founded by Raul Castro in the 1990s, GAESA controls a wide array of companies, ranging from the very profitable Gaviota S.A., which runs the island's tourist hotels, restaurants, car rentals and nightclubs, to TRD Caribe S.A., which runs all retail operations. In plain words: GAESA controls virtually every economic transaction in Cuba, making it -- by far -- the most powerful company in Cuba's totalitarian-command economy. It is run by Raul's son-in-law, General Luis Alberto Rodriguez Lopez- Callejas.

GAESA is the largest hotel company in Latin America. It controls more hotel rooms that the The Walt Disney Company. Thus, every tourist that stays at Cuba's famed Hotel Nacional, drinks a mojito at El Floridita and catches a show at The Tropicana, has one thing in common -- contributing to the Cuban military and security services bottom line.

These are the same Cuban armed forces that held a stolen U.S. Hellfire missile for nearly two years; that have recently been caught twice internationally-smuggling heavy weaponry, including the worst sanctions violations ever to North Korea; that oversee the most egregious abuses of human rights in the Western Hemisphere; that are subverting democracy in Venezuela and exporting surveillance systems and technology to other countries in the region; that welcome Russian military intelligence ships to dock in their ports; that share intelligence with the world's most dangerous anti-American regimes; and of which three senior Cuban military officers remain indicted in the United States for the murder of four Americans.

Surely you will hear from my fellow panelists today about Cuba's so-called "self-employment" sector, which some will refer to as the "private sector." First of all, the "self-employment" sector represents a very small part of the island's economy and it is important to understand its nature and limits. During economic crises, the Castro regime typically authorizes a host of services that Cubans can be licensed to provide, keeping at least a portion of what they may be paid. "Private enterprise" implies "private ownership." Yet Cuba's "self-employed" licensees have no ownership rights whatsoever - be it to their artistic or "intellectual" outputs, commodity they produce, or personal service they offer. Licensees have no legal entity (hence business) to transfer, sell or leverage. They don't even own the equipment essential to their self-employment. More to the point, licensees have no right to engage in foreign trade, seek or receive foreign investments. Effectually licensees continue to work for the state -- and when the state decides such jobs are no longer needed, licensees are shut down without recourse.

A central tenet of capitalism is recognition of property rights and it's precisely such rights that the Castro regime avoids through its distorted, licensing model. It's also why, despite these "self-employment" licenses, Cuba remains ranked 177 out of 178 nations in the world in the Index of Economic Freedom, a yearly joint compilation of The Wall Street Journal and The Heritage Foundation. Only North Korea is considered less economically free. It is not by coincidence that the Magna Carta preceded Adam Smith's Wealth of Nations – *not* vice-versa.

In sum, Cuba is a totalitarian dictatorship, where all business decisions are based on the political and control-based calculations of the Castro regime -- *not* on market forces. If the Cuban people enjoyed property rights to establish their businesses and were allowed to freely partake in foreign trade and investment – my testimony today would be very different.

Protect American Victims of Stolen Property

According to the Inter-American Law Review, the Castro regime's confiscation of U.S. assets was the "*largest uncompensated taking of American property by a foreign government in history*." Unfortunately, President Obama's policy of expanding business transactions with the Castro regime is already encouraging American companies to traffic and exploit properties stolen from other fellow Americans. Any expansion of such transactions by the U.S. Congress allowing bilateral trade, financing and investments with the Castro regime would further expose American victims. The Castro regime would be all-too-happy to "lease back" property stolen from one group of Americans to another group of Americans. But that would be a miscarriage of justice.

Meanwhile, Obama is denying any recourse, through his waiver of Title III of the 1996 Cuban Liberty and Democratic Solidarity Act ('Libertad'), to Americans who are seeing their property rights trampled upon. If the Obama Administration is unwilling to protect the rights of grieved Americans, then a private right of action should allow for the victims to do so directly through the rule of law.

As such, I would urge the U.S. Congress to pass legislation to end the President's waiver authority over Title III of the Libertad Act and grant Americans the legal standing to pursue justice. Moreover, any effort in the U.S. Congress tied to expanding business transactions with Castro regime -- beyond those currently authorized by statute – should have a mandatory Title III right of action attached to it.

Uphold U.S. Law and International Labor Norms

Lifting U.S. sanctions toward Cuba would also imply foreign investment. All foreign investment in Cuba must be done through minority joint ventures with Castro's military monopolies. Moreover, all workers in Cuba must be hired through the Castro regime's state-employment agency (Grupo Palco, S.A.), which in turn, pockets upwards of 92% of those workers' salaries. Recently, the Obama Administration issued a specific license to an Alabama tractor company (that has never built a tractor), Cleber LLC, to set up operations in the Cuban military's Mariel economic zone. This week, it also reportedly plans to allow Starwood Hotels to partner with the Cuban military to manage previously confiscated hotel properties. These deals are in *direct contravention* of the letter, spirit and intent of current U.S. law, as codified by statute. Regardless of your view of U.S. policy towards Cuba, the Congress should challenge such outright distortions of current

U.S. law by the Obama Administration. Moreover, these deals violate a myriad of international labor covenants, including:

- **Freedom of Association and Protection to Organize Convention** (No. 87) - Article 1(g) of Cuba's Labor Code grants workers "the right to associate themselves voluntarily and establish Unions." In practice, it is *not* allowed.

- **Protection of Wages Convention** (No. 05) - Cuba violates this Convention that prohibits deductions from wages with a view to insuring a direct or indirect payment for obtaining or retaining employment made to a state intermediary agency.

- **Right to Organize and Collective Bargaining Convention** (No. 98) - Collective bargaining is non-existent in Cuba.

- **Discrimination (Employment and Occupation) Convention** (No. 111) - By the Castro regime selecting the workers to supply to foreign investors, Cuba does not follow the mandate of equality of opportunity or treatment in employment and occupation.

- **Employment Policy Convention** (No. 122) - Cuba's policy of selecting who works where, regardless of skills or endowments, and transfers are not the result of the will of the worker.

- **The Universal Declaration of Human Rights** (Article 23) - Nonexistent in Cuba are: the right to work; free choice of employment; just and favorable working conditions; protection against unemployment; the right to equal pay for equal work; just and favorable remuneration; and the right to form and join trade unions.

Conclusion

There are many theories and estimates about how much more money one sector or another can make from conducting business with the Castro regime, if U.S. sanctions towards Cuba were further eased or lifted. Today, you'll surely hear many of those theories and estimates. However, as we've learned from the drastic drop in agricultural sales figures over the last year -- despite the Obama Administration easing sanctions and establishing diplomatic relations with the Castro regime -- that is hardly guaranteed. Moreover, any such theories must be weighed by serious factual considerations regarding the troubling structure of Cuba's business entities (military-run monopolies), its beneficiaries (the Castro family and regime cronies), the rights of its victims (both Cubans and Americans), and whether such practices are in the U.S.'s national interests.

Mr. POE. I thank the gentleman.

The Chair now recognizes Dr. Feinberg for his statement.

STATEMENT OF RICHARD E. FEINBERG, PH.D., PROFESSOR, SCHOOL OF GLOBAL POLICY AND STRATEGY, UNIVERSITY OF CALIFORNIA, SAN DIEGO

Mr. FEINBERG. Mr. Chairman, thank you very much for inviting me to participate in this most timely hearing on the eve of the historic visit to Cuba by President Barack Obama. May I ask that my full text, which I will just summarize now be entered into the record?

Mr. POE. Without objection.

Mr. FEINBERG. Thank you. The views here are solely my own and should not be attributed to other institutions. As U.S. relations with Cuba gradually normalize, Cuba will become an interesting if modest market for the U.S. economy but of considerable value for many individual U.S. businesses large and small and I will discuss some of these market opportunities.

But, as Jason Marczak has already emphasized, commerce with Cuba is about much more than the exchanges of grains and widgets. As the U.S. pivots toward a policy of positive engagement, economic exchange can be a potent political force.

Commercial exchange can also support broader U.S. objectives of advancing market-friendly economic reform, a more robust and independent private sector in Cuba and a thriving and diversified foreign investment presence.

Together, these changes make more likely—more likely the advance of fundamental U.S. interests in Cuba, the peaceful transition to a more pluralistic and prosperous Cuba to a Cuba more open to the world where the new normal is the free flow of goods, services, capital and ideas between our two nations.

Cuba today altogether imports about $14 billion in goods and services. For a small economy, that's a low import GDP ratio of only 17 percent.

Cuba cannot import more because it doesn't export to pay for those imports. But let's look ahead. Let us assume that Cuba accelerates its market-friendly economic reforms.

Let us assume that as part of that reform process Cuba's rates of capital investment rise, Cuban exports become more competitive and therefore Cuba's capacity to import expands. Let's assume that Cuban import growths is about 5 percent a year over a 10-year period.

If we take a compound rate of growth, sir, by 2027 Cuba will be importing $26 billion total, possibly as much as $34 billion.

What does that mean for U.S. producers? Given Cuba's geographic proximity and the complementarity between our two economies it is reasonable to project that U.S. exporters could capture 40 percent, perhaps, more of that expanded market.

U.S. businesses, as we've heard, are certainly well positioned to provide many of the agricultural and also industrial products that make up large portions of Cuba's current import requirements as well as the financial and professional services that a more dynamic Cuban economy will require.

By 2027, therefore, U.S. businesses could be selling $11 billion to $14 billion each year to Cuba. Over the 10-year period from 2018 post-Castro to 2027 U.S. businesses could sell during that 10-year period a cumulative $86 billion to $101 billion in goods and services to Cuba.

Cuba also desperately needs massive inflows of foreign investment. Cuba's domestic savings and investment ratio under 10 percent. The Latin American average is over 20 percent. Cuba must import more foreign investment to grow.

The Cuban Government has recognized that. It's advertized a list of 326 investment projects with an initial investment value exceeding $8 billion.

Cuba has said it has no particular objection to U.S. firms bidding on these opportunities, although it will seek a diversity of investment partners.

As we've already heard, many foreign firms from Europe, Latin America, Canada, China have already invested in Cuba. U.S. regulations, of course, prohibit U.S. firms from investing in Cuba. But eventually a new normal in cross-straits relations will witness many U.S. firms seizing these investment opportunities.

And Mr. Chairman, we know that U.S. investments abroad bring U.S. exports in their wake. Therefore, as the Cuban economy accelerates and U.S. investments—and U.S. businesses invest in Cuba, U.S. exports will also grow.

So therefore, my estimate of $11 billion to $14 billion in annual U.S. exports to Cuba a decade from now may prove to have been overly modest.

Now, just a brief word about the Cuba private sector. This is a very important part of our strategy. To date, the Cuban Government has authorized ½ million of its citizens to work in the self-employment private sector.

According to my calculations, as many as 1½ million additional Cubans have at least one foot in the private sector. That's as many as 2 million Cubans, 40 percent of their workforce compose the emerging private sector.

The U.S. is already a big piece of this emerging private sector in Cuba. U.S. investors are dining at private paladares, lodged at private guest homes and purchasing the creations of independent artisans, and remittances from the United States are driving many of these new businesses and they're allowing homeowners in Cuba to remodel their dwellings, employ private contractors and participate in the newly legal real estate market.

Cuba's emerging entrepreneurs and middle classes and by many measures, which I don't have time to go into today, Cuba is a middle class society.

These private entrepreneurs and middle class Cubans will seek a Cuba that is more normal, more like other societies in the Caribbean Basin where individuals have access to middle class consumption patterns and have ample opportunities to realize their talents, participate in public affairs and pursue their careers independent of state control.

Finally, Mr. Chairman, later this week President Obama and the First Lady will step foot on Cuban soil. President Obama will attempt to nudge the Cuban Government to press forward on their economic reforms with greater vigor.

But most important, I think, will be the messages that he delivers directly to the Cuban people. He will meet with the island's emerging entrepreneurs and middle class citizens.

He will engage with civil society and political dissidents.

Mr. POE. The gentleman's time has expired. The rest of your statement will be made part of the record.

Mr. FEINBERG. Thank you, sir. Thank you very much, Mr. Chair.

[The prepared statement of Mr. Feinberg follows:]

U.S. House of Representatives

Committee on Foreign Affairs

Subcommittee on Terrorism, Nonproliferation, and Trade

"Trade with Cuba: Growth and Opportunities"

March 15, 2016

Testimony

By Richard E. Feinberg

Professor, School of Public Policy and Strategy

University of California, San Diego

Thank you for inviting me to participate in this most timely hearing, on the eve of the historic visit to Cuba by President Barack Obama. Over the last five years, I have been researching and writing extensively on the Cuban economy. Change is coming slowly but inexorably, as Cuba gradually sheds its model of central planning and forges a mixed, hybrid variant of market socialism with a vibrant private sector, more open to global commerce and investment.

As U. S. relations with Cuba gradually normalize, Cuba will become an interesting if modest market for the U.S. economy but of considerable value for many individual U.S. businesses, large and small. I will discuss some of those market opportunities.

But commerce with Cuba is about much more than the mere exchange of grains and widgets. The US has waged economic warfare against Cuba for over 50 years, in an all-out effort to diminish and isolate the Cuban economy and to dislodge the government of Fidel Castro. As the U.S. pivots toward a policy of positive engagement, economic exchange can be a potent political force. This time, commercial exchange can support broader U.S. objectives of advancing market-friendly economic reform, a more robust and independent private sector, and a thriving and diversified foreign investment presence. Together, these changes do not guarantee the evolution of a political democracy, but they do make more likely the advancement of fundamental U.S. interests: the peaceful transition to a more pluralistic and prosperous Cuba, to a Cuba more open to the world, where the new normal is the free flow of goods, services, capital and ideas between our two nations.

Future Export Opportunities

Cuba imports about $14 billion (2014) in goods and services each year. For a small economy, in relation to the reported gross domestic product of $81 billion (2014), that's a low ratio of 17 percent. Since most Cuban products are not competitive on international markets, Cuban exports are well below potential capacity. This poor export performance constrains Cuba's ability to purchase products from the rest of the world.

Let us look ahead. Let us assume that Cuba proceeds with its market-friendly economic reforms – and hopefully accelerates the reform process. Let us also assume that as part of that reform process, Cuban rates of capital investment rise, Cuban exports become more competitive, and Cuba's capacity to import expands. Let us assume, therefore, that Cuban imports grow at 5 percent a year, over a ten year period (from 2018 to 2027). At a compound rate, by 2027, Cuba will be importing $26 billion. If the Cuban economy really takes off and imports grow at 7 percent a year, by 2027 Cuba will be importing $34 billion.

What does that mean for U.S. producers? Given Cuba's geographic proximity and the complementarities between our two economies, it is reasonable to project that U.S. exporters could capture 40 percent, and perhaps more, of that expanded market. U.S. businesses are certainly well positioned to provide many of the agricultural and industrial products that make up large portions of Cuba's current import requirements, as well as the financial and professional services that a more dynamic Cuban economy will require. By 2027, therefore, U.S. businesses could be selling $11 billion - $14 billion annually to Cuba, if Cuban imports grow 5 -7 percent per annum. **Over the ten years from 2018 – 2027, U.S. businesses could sell a cumulative $86 billion - $101 billion in goods and services to Cuba** (Table 1).

Even with this higher growth, the Cuban market is too modest to make a marked impact on the overall U.S. balance of payments. These projections do suggest, however, that an expanding Cuban market could make a real difference for many individual U.S. businesses.

We should recognize, of course, that such a bright scenario implies a reciprocal opening of the U.S. market to Cuban exports of goods and services. Already U.S. travelers are purchasing Cuban hospitality services. U.S. consumers will also benefit from renowned Cuban brands of rum and cigars. But a more competitive Cuban economy, fully integrated into global supply chains, will eventually produce a wide area of agricultural and industrial products, quite possibly including healthy organic foods, new life-saving medicines, computer software, and wonderful artistic creations, among many others. Eventually, we can imagine Cuba joining an existing free-trade area, such as the U.S.-Central America FTA (CAFTA-DR), which includes regional partners as well as the United States. Certainly, Cuba will no longer be the only nation in the world (other than North Korea) that remains outside of the multilateral financial institutions: the International Monetary Fund, the World Bank, and the regional Inter-American Development Bank.[1]

Table 1. Potential US Exports to Cuba (USD – billions)

	2018	2027	Cumulative 2018 - 2027
Cuban imports growth at 5% p.a.	6.8	10.6	85.6
Cuban imports growth at 7% p.a.	7.3	13.5	101.4

Source: Author's calculations

Foreign Investment Projects

Cuba desperately needs massive inflows of foreign investment. Cuba's domestic savings and investment rates are under 10 percent, whereas the Latin American average exceeds 20 percent. The only way for Cuba to close its formidable investment gap is through foreign investment. Foreign investment will bring not only badly needed capital but also modern technology, management techniques and access to international credits and product markets.

---

[1] Richard E. Feinberg, *Reaching Out: Cuba's New Economy and the International Response* (Brookings, Latin American Initiative, 2011).

The Cuban government recognizes its need for foreign capital. Last year it advertised a "Portfolio of Opportunities for Foreign Investment" that compiled 326 specific projects with an initial investment value exceeding $8 billion. The potential projects range over most of the Cuban economy. Not surprisingly, the most robust sector is tourism, at 94 potential projects. Other sectors included oil (86 projects), agriculture and agro-industry (40 projects), renewable energy (22 projects), industry (21), transportation (15 projects), construction (14 projects), biotechnology and medicine (9 projects), business (4 projects), health (3 projects), and audiovisual (3 projects).

Cuba has said that it has no particular objection to U.S. firms bidding on these opportunities, although it will seek a diversity of investment partners. Many foreign firms, mainly from Europe and Latin America but also from Canada and China, have already invested in Cuba. Well-known brands such as the Spanish Melía hotel chain, the Swiss conglomerate Nestlé, the Canadian mining and energy firm Sherritt International, and the British-Dutch multinational Unilever have long been active in the Cuban market.[2] Imperial Tobacco markets Cuban cigars and Pernod Ricard markets premium Cuban rum.

U.S. regulations, of course, have prohibited U.S. firms from investing in Cuba. Eventually, a new normal in cross-Straits relations will witness many U.S. firms seizing these investment opportunities, whether as wholly-owned foreign investments or as joint ventures with Cuban state-owned enterprises.

We know that U.S. investments abroad bring U.S. exports in their wake. As the Cuban economy accelerates and U.S. businesses invest, U.S. exports will also grow. The mix of U.S. exports – manufacturing, agriculture, services – will expand to include a widening array of U.S. firms. **If U.S. investors begin to compete in the Cuban market, my estimates of $11 - 14 billion in U.S. annual exports to Cuba a decade from now may prove to have been overly modest.**

The Cuban Private Sector and Emerging Middle Classes

To date, the Cuban government has authorized half a million citizens to work in the "self-employment" private sector. According to my calculations, as many as another 1.5 million

---

[2] Richard E. Feinberg, *The New Cuban Economy: What Roes for Foreign Investment?* (Brookings, Latin American Initiative, December 2012).

Cubans work at least part time in private enterprise. Thus, as many as 2 million individuals, or 40 percent of the labor force, compose the emerging private sector.[3] These hard-working Cubans make up one of the future key pillars of a dynamic Cuban economy where the state sector, while still dominant, makes room for an increasingly pluralistic economic system.

The United States is already a big piece of this story of an emerging private sector in Cuba. U.S. visitors are dining at private *paladares*, lodging at private guest houses, and purchasing the creations of independent artisans. Remittances from the United States are driving many of the new businesses, and are allowing homeowners to remodel their dwellings, employ private contractors, and participate in the newly legal real estate market.

The administration has authorized U.S. firms to sell to these private entrepreneurs, although the Cuban government has yet to establish the channels through which such trade could flow. This auto-embargo ill serves the Cuban people. Now that the administration has also authorized U.S. sales to certain state-owned enterprises, perhaps the Cuban government will open pathways for trade with its legal private sector as well.

By many measures, Cuba is a middle-class society. The majority of Cubans have at least ten years of formal education, Cuban women participate actively in the labor market, Cuban fertility rates are the lowest in the Western Hemisphere, and most Cubans own their own homes and benefit from a broad if leaky social safety net. But there is one measure whereby Cuba would certainly not qualify as middle class: access to individual consumer items. Most Cubans lack what middle-class Americans take for granted: modern household appliances, rapid internet connections, an automobile with a reliable engine.

Cuba's emerging entrepreneurs and middle classes aspire to greater economic opportunity, individual autonomy, and material prosperity. It may be overly mechanical to predict that these Cuban middle classes will demand democratic capitalism, but it is safe to imagine that they will seek a Cuba that is more normal, more like other societies in the Caribbean basin where individuals have access to middle-class consumption patterns and have ample opportunities to realize their talents, participate in public affairs, and pursue their careers independent of state control.

---

[3] Richard E. Feinberg, *Soft Landing in Cuba? Emerging Entrepreneurs and Middle Classes* (Brookings, Latin American Initiative. November 2013)

The Aspirations of Cuban Millennials

In my forthcoming book, *Open for Business: Building the New Cuban Economy*, I converse with a dozen Cuban millennials. Every one approved of the decisions by Barack Obama and Raúl Castro to normalize diplomatic relations. They expressed hope that economic relations normalize as well, allowing the free flow of goods, capital, and people across the Florida Straits. In some respects, the Cuban millennials are similar to their counterparts around the world: alert, ambitious, hard-working, cosmopolitan in outlook and interested in world travel, measuring their own creativity and results against global standards. Some have already opened their own businesses, others are improving their English in anticipation of working closely with U.S. businesses. For these dozen millennials, normal relations with the United States imply a powerful U.S. influence on the island. But Cubans also want to preserve their "Cubanismo," the unique national identity that blends centuries of complex interactions of many civilizations – refashioned and improved to meet the exigencies of the twenty-first century.

By bolstering the Cuban private sector and middle classes, and by giving hope to the millennials, the United States can help to create conditions for a soft landing for Cuba, a gradual shift toward a more open and prosperous future. Similarly, once U.S. firms are allowed to invest in Cuba, they too will become a window to the world.

The Visit of President Obama

Later this week, President Obama and the First Lady will step foot on Cuban soil. Other U.S. presidents have visited the island, to attend an international conference (Coolidge), or prior to their presidency to battle the Spanish (Teddy Roosevelt) or to vacation (John F. Kennedy). But President Obama will be the first to expressly visit Cuba for an official state visit.

President Obama will attempt to nudge the Cuban government to press forward on their economic reforms with more vigor. But more important will be the messages that he delivers directly to the Cuban people. Obama will meet with the island's emerging entrepreneurs and middle class citizens, he will engage with civil society and political dissidents. He will attend a baseball game between the Tampa Bay Rays and the Cuban national team. He may find additional ways to mix with the Cuban people who will receive him, it can be safely predicted, with overwhelming enthusiasm.

Our president will be able to draw on his extraordinary rhetorical skills to paint a vision of a new Cuba where citizens freely exercise their chosen professions, engage directly with a transparent and accountable government, have access to the global internet, and travel abroad routinely for family and business purposes. This vision of a brighter future can be attractive enough to motivate Cubans, especially its ambitious and talented millennials, to remain on the island and for the resourceful Cuban American diaspora to invest in that vision.

In this new normal, U.S. firms and investors will engage freely in Cuba, to the benefit of the American economy and the Cuban people. Let there be no doubt, this day will come. The only question is the date of its arrival.

Mr. POE. The Chair will now recognize himself for questions. Then we'll let the members of the panel or the dais make comments and questions. Thank you once again, gentlemen, for being here.

It seems to me that the U.S. policy against Cuba, the Castro regime, as articulated by Mr. Claver-Carone, a lot of reasons why the Government of Cuba is not acting appropriately by international standards.

We cannot solve all those problems here today. Maybe we can talk about one of those, which is normalizing relationships regarding the issue of trade.

It seems to me that Cuba trades with everybody in the hemisphere except us. They get their rice from Vietnam. Happens to still be a communist country.

And getting rice from Vietnam that they consume I do not understand how that punishes the Castro regime by not letting us sell agricultural goods to Cuba with Vietnam as a competitor. It would just seem to me that that doesn't punish the Cubans. It helps the Vietnamese and it punishes the United States.

Now, Mr. Claver-Carone has talked about some changes in U.S. policy that actually, because of the changes, agricultural sales to Cuba and specifically rice dropped as opposed to increased.

Now, I'd like you all to weigh in on this. Mr. Marczak, can you weigh in on this issue that Mr. Claver-Carone mentioned? U.S. changes its policy and the policy doesn't help trade.

It reduces trade, and how did that affect the Cuban Government on dealing with us because of that change in policy in 2004 or 2005, whichever it was?

Would you explain that specifically, please?

Mr. MARCZAK. Chairman Poe, thank you for the question.

I think that we have to look at the, first of all, the decrease in agricultural exports to Cuba, which is not a result of the President's—President Obama's actions but it's a result of a number of different factors on the island and also a result, as my colleagues on the panel have mentioned—a result of the lack of competitiveness that our agricultural——

Mr. POE. Lack of what?

Mr. MARCZAK. Lack of competitiveness.

Mr. POE. Okay.

Mr. MARCZAK. That our agricultural exporters have in so far as exporting their products to Cuba when looked at comparison to other countries around the world.

As you mentioned, Mr. Chairman, Vietnam is a prime example of that. It's a country that is taking advantage of the fact that the U.S. should naturally be the number-one agricultural exporter to Cuba.

But because of the restrictions that lay in U.S. law including restrictions that Congress could potentially modify, the United States——

Mr. POE. Let me interrupt a minute. We trade with Vietnam, do we not?

Mr. MARCZAK. Yes, we do.

Mr. POE. And Vietnam, like other countries, have human rights violations that we're concerned about as a nation, correct?

Mr. MARCZAK. That's correct.

Mr. POE. Continue.

Mr. MARCZAK. That's correct. And I would also say that our opening with—trade with Vietnam has allowed for an opening and a degree of liberty in Vietnam.

Obviously, Vietnam remains a communist country but we see the result of an opening of trade with Vietnam in so far as providing greater economic liberties and opening the door for political liberties to the Vietnamese.

So, in conclusion, in answer to your question, Mr. Chairman, you know, the policy that Congress has the ability to change and policy that could be changed, I think, without a lot of political cost specifically in the agricultural sector could allow U.S. agricultural exporters to be more competitive and to also ensure that the Cubans, you know, get their agricultural products and help to create jobs here in the United States rather than creating jobs back in Vietnam.

Mr. POE. Specifically, what change could be made? I know Congress can—has to be the one to lift the embargo but what are you talking about regarding the financial situation of cash on demand as opposed to credit, letting the agricultural community assume the risk rather than prohibiting it completely? Delve into that specifically in the remaining time that you have?

Mr. MARCZAK. Yes. Specifically, Congress could—the administration has allowed for the financing of exports in a range of sectors through executive action.

But Congress has the sole authority because of Helms-Burton to be able to remove the restrictions that prohibit agricultural export financing, and without that financing and, as you suggest, that financing—the risk for that financing could be taken by the exporters themselves. But without the ability to provide financing for those agricultural products our exporters and our products are at an inherent disadvantage.

Mr. POE. All right. My time has expired.

I'll recognize the gentleman from Massachusetts, Mr. Keating.

Mr. KEATING. Thank you, Mr. Chairman.

Sunday's New York Times included an article that highlighted the United States' and Cuba's different visions of economic engagement and we touched on some of these things.

But tourism has long satisfied Cuba's need for foreign currency and it's clear that there remains a stark disparity between the willingness of Cuban businesses or authorities to enter into trade with the United States companies and the desire of our domestic business people to do so.

One statistic in that article that was cited by the president of U.S.-Cuba Trade and Economic Council—he said that he counted 500 visits to Cuba by American business people since December 2014, more than 140 visits by United States representatives and officials but he can count on the number of—count on his fingers, you know, just the business deals that had been reached.

Meanwhile, Cuban officials repeatedly just point to the trade embargo as an example of the United States' lack of commitment to strengthen relations.

I'd just like to—and we touched on some of these things but give everyone a chance—how would you explain this lagging growth of trade between U.S. and Cuba? What other things that we haven't touched on to explain that lack of growth, given the trade restrictions? Mr. Feinberg?

Mr. CLAVER-CARONE. I'll take a stab. I'd be happy to take a stab because I think it ties into both of these questions.

You know, the issue here, if we were talking here about trade with the Cuban people, as a matter of fact even trade with Vietnam where there are private entities that you can be involved with trade with, it's a whole different story, you know, because it's not politicized trade.

Trade with Cuba is all politicized because there's only one customer. If that were to change, my testimony would have been very different today.

But the fact is our sales and what the Castro regime is doing with—particularly with what you notice is essentially trying to coerce the U.S. business community to pursue its geopolitical gains—its needs, in the same way that it took an American hostage in order to gain—to coerce the United States into releasing three spies including one that was serving two life sentences for the murder—for murder conspiracy of some Americans and now wants to coerce the business community in order to unilaterally finance its regime.

And I think that that right there is the fundamental problem here—the fundamental difference with Vietnam. The fundamental also difference with Vietnam and Brazil and the sales to them is that those are essentially subsidized by the state, by entities and deals that are less than transparent in which the state is essentially financing those completely.

I mean, we're not even going to be able to compete with those deals in that regards because it's all politicized and that's the problem. When that opens up, then we can have a different picture and a different story.

Mr. KEATING. Is there any—some people have suggested that there's a deliberate effort reducing imports to the United—you know, from the United States to increase political pressure on the United States for additional sanction easing measures. Do you think there's any truth to that, Dr. Feinberg?

Mr. FEINBERG. So I think, first, in terms of limitations on our side, up until a few weeks ago, U.S. exporters were only permitted to export to the emerging small-scale private sector in Cuba.

So we were still not allowed to export to the state-owned enterprises which still make up 80 percent of production in Cuba, okay, so that was a big no on our part.

And with regard to investment, many U.S. firms when down there thinking about investment. That is totally off the table because of U.S. sanctions still to this day. Okay. So we have those restrictions on our side.

Now, on the Cuban side, we have said the small-scale private enterprise we are happy to sell to you. There is where the Cubans have been dragging their feet and I would suggest a couple of reasons for that.

One is ideological. They tend to prefer the state-owned enterprises as still socialists. So they don't like us preferring and giving advantage to the small-scale private sector.

Now, most recently the Obama administration did say okay, U.S. firms under certain conditions can also sell to state-owned enterprises.

So we'll see now when President Obama is down in Havana if he'll be able to say okay, we gave you something that you were pushing for—now open channels for U.S. firms to sell to the emerging private sector in Cuba, and I hope very much he can bring home that concession from Cuba.

Mr. KEATING. Well, let me take it a step further. Let's assume that result. Are they going to still—because they have this ideology, are they going to still try and limit the activity with the private side? They're going to continue to do that even more so maybe?

Mr. FEINBERG. Well, so they've allowed, as I mentioned, 500,000 in the private sector so far. There are still all sorts of limitations.

The President will be meeting with a group of these private sector entrepreneurs, I understand. I think we'll have a—he will have a dialogue with them. He'll listen, what are your major problems.

Mr. KEATING. You think there's an ideology there so this is being manipulated?

Mr. FEINBERG. It's a combination of ideology and power. I mean, the government—power comes through the control of the economy and the state-owned enterprises. That causes them to want to limit the growth of the small-scale enterprises, without a doubt.

Mr. KEATING. That's interesting. Thank you. I yield back.

Mr. POE. The Chair recognizes the gentleman from Pennsylvania, Mr. Perry.

Mr. PERRY. Thank you, Mr. Chairman.

I hate to be the guy that doesn't want to join the Cuba lovefest here but I need to associate my remarks with Mr. Claver-Carone.

And then that I'm probably not going to talk about trade here. I got a couple statements to make and I know you're all interested in making money and that's great. So am I.

From General James Clapper, director of national intelligence, last month, the threat from foreign intelligence entities is persistent, complex and evolving. Targeting and collection of U.S. political, military, economic and technical information by foreign intelligence services continues unabated. Russia and China pose the greatest threat followed by Iran and Cuba.

I'll just remind you that something you all know, they're about 100 miles off the coast of Florida, right. Two weeks prior the U.S. military Southern Command held its annual Caribbean regional security conference.

Senior members of Castro's KGB-trained spy agency were invited to participate. I find that particularly irritating and self-destructive as a person who served decades now in the United States military.

I also want to remind you of the listening posts, the largest ones in the world based at Lourdes, which is sponsored by Russia and reopened after we brought Cuba to their knees financially and the Soviet Union as well and forced them to close it at some point but reopened, and the one by China at Bao Cao.

I would also like to remind you that Cuba's—this is from the Cuban—the state-sponsored newspaper, Cuba's communist propaganda newspaper, Granma, has published an article claiming that

President Obama's scheduled visit to Havana in March dispels decades of evidence that the Cuban Government violates the human rights of its citizens on the very weekend in which Cuban state police arrested almost 200 dissidents for peaceful marches against communism.

And I'd further like to remind you of recent arrests of U.S. State Department officials—an official and his wife for over 30 years of spying at the State Department named Walter and Gwen Myers as well as Ana Montes, who worked for the Defense Intelligence Agency as a United States citizen, as a Cuban spy.

While you all might like to dance with the devil to make a couple bucks, you can be—and with all due respect to Dr. Weinberg when you said they prefer the socialist model—I'll remind you, as you probably well know that socialism is an economic construct. Communism is the political construct that forces the economic construct.

These folks in power have no interest at all in changing their ways and they are going to use us and our foolishness, our generosity to further their intentions.

And while you all might be happy that we have a socialist running for the presidency of the United States, I find it particularly vexing that American service members spent and pledged their lives and often gave their lives in the fight against exactly that.

And now we're saying yet again it's great to engage with these folks in the hope—in the hope that they will change after 40 or 50 years.

I don't know what delusion you folks are under but listen, if you're under one that's great but do me this favor and I would hope that the President would do us this favor as well, which is if you're going to make a deal when a deal's been made let's find out what we're getting up front as opposed to giving everything away and then hoping that we'll get something on the other side.

And so with that I will ask one question—one question only. Anybody can answer it. Everybody can answer it. What did we get—specifically, tangibly, what did we get for the deal that we just made?

Mr. MARCZAK. I'm happy to take the first response to that.

Thank you, Congressman, for your question. I think, first of all, I think I'm not trying to dance with the devil to make a few bucks here, right.

I'm the director of the Latin American Growth Initiative at a nonpartisan think tank here. I have no skin in the game in so far as cash on this.

But I think what we have to look at insofar as what is the—what is the best way to seek greater political and economic liberties for the Cuban people. I think that that's——

Mr. PERRY. I'm with you. Economic is one of the powers that we have. But I wonder what we're getting, what we have gotten for the deal.

Mr. MARCZAK. Yes.

Mr. PERRY. We gave in—we already gave, right? So what do we get? What do we hope to get?

68

Mr. MARCZAK. Yes. Yes. I would say there's a few things that
we've—well, first of all, I think there's a few things that we've gotten from the actions of the last 15 months.

One is that on a geostrategic perspective we've increased the
power, the positioning of the United States and our perception
among our allies not just across the hemisphere—countries that
are incredibly important for us to work with.

Our policy toward Cuba has been the thorn in our side insofar
as seeking greater relationships across Latin America, encoun-
tering other regimes that I think that we would be in agreement
with that we also want to—that are also restricting the ability of
their people to express their political liberties including that regime
in Caracas, Venezuela.

Mr. PERRY. If I may ask you, with your indulgence, Mr. Chairman, which Latin American countries have we increased our stance
with by—via our position with Cuba now? Which Latin American
countries?

Mr. MARCZAK. I would say we have increased our stance with
Brazil, with Argentina, with Colombia, with probably Mexico. I
would say most countries in the hemisphere had gotten to the point
that they could no longer defend our policy.

Now, insofar as what does that mean for the Castros, right—
what does this—our policy should not be one that keeps the Castros in power. Our policy should be one that seeks to provide greater liberties for the Cuban people.

And I would contend that over the last five-plus decades our embargo has been the crutch and the answer for the Castro regime
of why the country is continuously suffering from economic ills.

Whenever there's a problem in Cuba the answer is it's because
of the embargo. Now, obviously the embargo still remains in place
but by chipping away at some of the—some of the restrictions in
our policy we're taking away bit by bit the reasons in which the
Castro regime can blame others from the outside, specifically the
imperialists from the United States, for the economic problems that
they have in their own country.

Mr. PERRY. Thank you, Mr. Chairman, I yield.

Mr. POE. The other four gentleman may submit their answer for
the record in writing to Mr. Perry's question. I understand we're
going to have votes very soon.

So I'll recognize the gentlelady from California, Ms. Bass.

Ms. BASS. Thank you, Mr. Chair.

I think my questions are from a little slightly different direction
there but with all due respect to my colleague over there.

You know, I have had problems for many years with the U.S.
policy directed to Cuba and our policy with regime change through
the embargo, to me, has really hurt U.S. businesses.

And I appreciate you describing from the agricultural industry
ways that you could certainly expand your business if, you know,
we were to remove the remaining barriers.

I have also always resented the fact that my freedom was denied
to travel wherever I choose to travel regardless of what regime
might be in power. I have resented the fact that my own country
prohibited me from travelling to where I would like to go.

I had mentioned before that I wanted to talk about health care and I do have a question for you about agriculture as well.

You know, the Cubans have invented a vaccine that helps with lung cancer and there is also a medical product that they have a medication that helps reduce the need to amputate for diabetics.

Diabetics—the lead cause of feet amputation in the United States and probably many other countries is diabetes and the Cubans have a medication that helps with that.

And so one question I have for Dr. Feinberg is do you think that the President could issue a general authorization for Cuban-developed pharmaceutical and other medical products?

The problem is, as I understand it, is that we are allowing this medication, which is called Heberprot—we are allowing it to be tested—clinical trials in the United States.

But we will not give a company the ability to market it and no company in the world is going to invest the expense into a clinical trial unless they have the ability to market the drug as well.

So I want to know, given the current restrictions, if you think that that might—you know, that the President might be able to issue that.

And then to Mr. Stoesser from the—from the Texas Rice Council, you know, one of the other things that I think our companies as well as the Cubans could benefit by is our scientific technology—our scientific knowledge, farming technology and farm equipment in terms of sales.

And then I believe Dr. Feinberg said that there is already a restriction that our commerce in agriculture has to be with small farmers. I think that that's what you were saying.

So those are the questions I would propose—I would pose to Dr. Feinberg and also to Mr. Stoesser.

Mr. FEINBERG. So just to clarify, so my general comment about U.S. sales was for all products other than agriculture.

Ms. BASS. Oh, I see.

Mr. FEINBERG. Which has separate legislation, and some medicines. So I think when President Obama goes down there we will see the warmth of the Cuban people.

Ms. BASS. Oh, by the way, I'm going on a trip. So thank you for telling me about what I'm going to experience when I'm there in terms of meeting with small farmers. Go ahead.

Mr. FEINBERG. Okay. Excellent. Well, I think then you also will experience the warmth of the Cuban people and their admiration and appreciation for the President of the United States and for Americans in general, and that is one result of the people-to-people diplomacy that has been going on for the last several years as a result of the relaxation of certain sanctions.

As you point out, Cuba has a very active biotechnology sector. They have developed these various vaccines, as you point out.

Now, for them to be marketed in the U.S., of course, they have to go through clinical trials. As you may know, the Roswell Cancer Center in New York is working on the lung vaccine, which seems promising but, of course, we have to be sure that it's effective and safe.

I do completely agree with your basic point that the United States ought to say in general with regard to medicines which are, after all, lifesaving—a very obvious humanitarian product, that if they pass FDA regulations ought to be available to American——

Ms. BASS. Humanitarian for us.

Mr. FEINBERG. Precisely. For us, on our side. Yes. So humanitarian.

Now, I think there, there is the additional element, however, that the Cuban Government has been hesitant to allow joint ventures or even licensing to not only U.S. but international pharmaceutical companies in general, and that's another area where one has to recognize that the timidity of the Cuban state—their lack of knowledge and their fear of global markets—is something that they're going to have to gradually work their way through. But we can encourage them in that regard.

Ms. BASS. Thank you.

Mr. POE. The gentlelady yields back her time.

Mr. Stoesser, you'll have to put that in writing, the answer to her question.

The Chair recognizes the gentleman from Arkansas, Mr. Crawford.

Mr. CRAWFORD. Thank you, Mr. Chairman.

To Mr. Stoesser and to Dr. Rosson, my understanding of the cash in advance rules have been rewritten again to be less restrictive. But there's been no noticeable improvement to rice exports to Cuba.

Do you believe the Treasury Department's reinterpretation of the rules will have any impact on our competitiveness in Cuba or will our ag export posture remain weak until exporters are able to offer credit to Cuban importers?

Mr. STOESSER. It's my understanding that commodities were not included in that recent ruling, only tractors and telecommunication things but not agricultural commodities.

Mr. CRAWFORD. Okay.

Mr. STOESSER. And I think that rule needs to be changed to include commodities, of course.

Mr. CRAWFORD. Sure. Dr. Rosson, the U.S. poultry sector has seemed to find ways to have a stronger export presence in Cuba. What's keeping other ag industries from implementing a similar framework?

Mr. ROSSON. Well, I think when we look at the overall commodities situation globally today, things like nickel, for example, those prices are at near historic lows and that affects the ability of the Cubans to generate enough foreign exchange to purchase products.

Now, what's different about much of the poultry that we export there it's largely leg quarters, which are sold at a discount relative to other cuts of poultry. So therefore they naturally have a competitive advantage.

Where we tend to lose is the fact that we don't offer credit—that our payment terms are somewhat restrictive. And so by the time we transfer funds around the—between Cuba, a third country, back to the United States, we've lost time and as a result we have vessels that are held up and being charged extra money because of those delays in shipping and the Cubans bear that cost and the result is they tend to turn elsewhere for some of their supplies.

Mr. CRAWFORD. You conclude that food and ag exports have the potential to exceed $1 billion annually but even stronger exports can be achieved through further infrastructure improvement investment. To what extent do you believe that U.S. direct investment in the private Cuban agribusiness would strengthen our export posture?

Mr. ROSSON. I think investment is absolutely crucial. My experience of having been there several times over the last number of years port infrastructure, road infrastructure needs improvement.

I've had personal experience working with companies that were exporting frozen foods into the Cuban market and we'd have a power outage and those frozen desserts would melt, then they'd refreeze and you take those out and display them at a food show and you run into problems trying to sell your product.

So infrastructure is crucial. Reliable power, good infrastructure, improvements in all load, off load capability. The port is important, and then another aspect is business development. We have not been active in business development there because we've been precluded.

Now we do have the opportunity to do that and by business development I'm talking about working with the private sector individually to try and improve their capacity to do business and develop their economy on a fairly small scale in the beginning but which has the potential to grow, and as that growth occurs we would see incomes rise and we would see improvement in the Cuban consumer's ability to buy food.

Mr. CRAWFORD. Mr. Marczak, do you believe that American investment in private Cuban agribusiness might help accelerate privatization in the Cuban ag sector?

Mr. MARCZAK. Yes. I believe that the Cuban—what the Cuban private sector needs is more investment from outside, right. I think that there's a few things.

One is that—you know, that includes fully lifting the remittance cap as well so the Cubans—the small businesses in Cuba can have access to the necessary financing and investment that would be—that is critical for their long-term survival and I think as well the agriculture sector, specifically the growth in the number of agricultural cooperatives, has been a real success insofar as the incremental.

Again, we have to look at success in measured terms. This is only a few years after a long policy of completely closed off. But it's an area in which there is—it's ripe for further engagement from the private sector and private sector growth.

Mr. CRAWFORD. Do you think that U.S. investment might help reduce the Castro regime's role in the Cuban economy more quickly than maintain our current isolationist posture?

Mr. MARCZAK. I believe that current—I believe that investment—the more investment from the U.S. the more jobs that creates in the Cuban private sector, the fewer Cubans are dependent upon the state for their jobs and the more Cubans can express their free will without the potential recourse of losing their only income.

Mr. CRAWFORD. Thank you. I yield back.

Mr. POE. The Chair recognizes the gentleman from Minnesota, Mr. Emmer.

Mr. EMMER. Thank you, Mr. Chair, and thanks to the witnesses for being here today.

Mr. Claver-Carone, when's the last time that you visited Cuba?

Mr. CLAVER-CARONE. The Castro regime, as you know, has a list of 100,000 Cubans at least that they don't allow——

Mr. EMMER. Mr. Claver-Carone, reclaiming my time.

Mr. CLAVER-CARONE. They don't—they don't give me a visa. They don't give me a visa.

Mr. EMMER. When's the last time that you've been there?

Mr. CLAVER-CARONE. When I was a little kid because they don't give me a visa because people that are critical of the Castro regime don't get a visa because I think that's important to know.

Mr. EMMER. Thank you. Thank you very much. Reclaiming my time.

I find it interesting when you talk about what's happening in Cuba because if you had been there recently you would see that the Castros, they live in what I would describe as suburban Dallas—a nice neighborhood with boulevards and well-manicured lawns and nice big homes and the rest of the population they don't live in—well, I would say they do live in very underwhelming circumstances and that would leave one to believe when they see it firsthand and they experience that whether the embargo is in place or not the Castros are going to do just fine. It's actually more about the Cuban people when we talk about trade.

This is a mutual relationship with value on both sides, and I guess I think when you talk about the issues of religious freedoms and other humanitarian concerns they're real and I don't have any doubt maybe to the degree and where they're happening but I think we can agree that that's still real.

The fact is, however, that these have existed now for 55 years and the embargo has been in place actually more than 55 years. The embargo has been in place for 55 years. It hasn't changed.

The definition of insanity, I've been taught, is doing the same thing over and over and over and expecting a different result, and I'm not even going to bother to ask how you think that the current state of economic sanctions is going to change something in the next 55 years.

Instead, I think I want to turn to Mr. Marczak and ask when it comes to the embargo it was initially put in place as a policy to isolate the Castro regime and to destabilize the Castro regime so that ultimately the Cuban people could self-determine once again and enter into these agreements that we're talking about, this growth opportunity.

But in fact, Mr. Marczak, isn't it true that what's happened is the policy has isolated the United States. It hasn't isolated Cuba because Cuba's doing business with everybody around the world and everybody in the Western Hemisphere with the exception of the United States, correct?

Mr. MARCZAK. Correct, Congressman, and I'm sure that you've seen when you've been to Cuba as well the number of foreign Embassies across Havana.

Cuba has more foreign Embassies than any country in the Western Hemisphere outside of the United States. So Cuba has successfully used the embargo and the isolation and destabilizing intention of the embargo to claim an outsized role insofar as geopolitical posturing and insofar as its place not only in the global affairs but as a leader in the global south.

Mr. EMMER. So talking about growth then—trade and growth— right now the question is not really about whether Cuba is going to be able to do business because there are entrepreneurs from all over the world rushing into Cuba right now as we speak because of the President's unilateral action to start to relax whatever the administration can outside of Helms-Burton.

The question really is whether or not the United States entrepreneurs will have that same opportunity. Isn't that correct, Mr. Marczak?

Mr. MARCZAK. That is correct. There's a real concern that because of the—if we have this opening of regulations the rest of the world sees the writing on the wall that our policy and the embargo is eventually going to be lifted.

Mr. EMMER. So lastly—I mean, I heard one of my colleagues talk about China and Russia and Iran. I mean, isn't the risk that those types of players will move in to Cuba and isn't that—isn't that really what's happened with our foreign policy since the 1950s, that our policy literally pushed this regime to Russia and don't we risk that again?

Mr. MARCZAK. Yes. You correctly state that Russia has been the fall back for the Cubans at times of economic uncertainty. The Chinese are looking at increasing their investments in Cuba.

Mr. EMMER. Thank you.

Lastly, Mr. Stoesser, thank you so much for being here. I just want to clarify, you aren't just in the business of agriculture to make money with a 100-year business.

I take it you have some pride in feeding the world with what you do?

Mr. STOESSER. I sure do. I want my sons and grandsons to be able to do what I did because they love it, too. I love to farm.

Mr. EMMER. Thank you.

Mr. STOESSER. I need to have it return.

Mr. EMMER. Thank you. I yield back.

Mr. POE. The Chair will recognize the gentleman from California, Mr. Sherman. We are voting so if the gentleman would be precise.

Mr. SHERMAN. I know that another colleague asked Mr. Claver-Carone whether—when was the last time you were in Cuba. I assume that the last time you were in Cuba would have been the last time that you would be a free man.

One of my colleagues tried to get me to go to the Gaza Strip and I had to explain to him that my record was not in accord with that of Hamas.

Biggest opportunity for Cuba is tourism. Is there any—I would evidence that we're going to increase the total amount that Americans have to spend on their vacations or if Americans spend money on their vacations in Cuba they won't be spending it elsewhere.

Mr. Claver-Carone, is there—would this just pull tourist dollars away from Puerto Rico, the Virgin Islands, Florida and other tourist destinations in the United States?

Mr. CLAVER-CARONE. I always say that first and foremost if you're looking for a tourist destination Miami Beach is basically going to help our economy a lot better or Cape Cod or California has beautiful beaches and things of that sort. So I believe we should support our economy. But I think the important thing is——

Mr. SHERMAN. And even if you do want to go to a foreign country you can go to how many different Caribbean countries are there who will then buy U.S. products on fair terms?

Mr. CLAVER-CARONE. Absolutely, and the whole concept that we hear so much with agricultural trade is that we want U.S. tourists to go over there so then there's a demand created for more products from here from the United States.

But essentially we're feeding the same American mouth whether we feed it in Miami Beach or we feed it in Barrero Beach. I think it's essentially the same product.

But I think that brings to an important point is the reason we have these travel-related, tourism-related transactions in Cuba is because it's the Cuban military and security services' number one source of income. The Cuban military is the largest hotel owners in Latin America. They own more hotel rooms than the Walt Disney World Company. We sanction tourism toward Cuba and we sanction oil to Iran for a reason, because one is the number one source of income versus that of another.

Mr. SHERMAN. There are, I think, 6,000 certified U.S. claims where the Cuban Government has appropriated American assets. Does Cuba have any interest in settling any of those claims?

Mr. CLAVER-CARONE. Not that I'm aware of in that regards. They like to talk a lot and we see that there's a lot of talk and I think in that regards we need to consider, as I mention in my testimony, the rights of Americans.

President Obama and President Bush and President Clinton before him had always waived Title III of the Libertad Act that provided a right of action for American victims of that.

But now if we're going to allow investment in essentially for the Castro regime to lease back to us our own stolen property then we should perhaps consider having a prior right of action as is current law in order for the American victims of this trafficked property to be able to receive compensation.

Mr. SHERMAN. Let me ask the other witnesses, in order to export agricultural items to Cuba will it be necessary for us to provide the financing?

Mr. FEINBERG. So let me say I think that, first of all, in general Cuba does state to state credits. They seek soft bland credits when possible. That's basically what lies behind, for example——

Mr. SHERMAN. So in order to export the Cubans are going to ask the U.S. Government to—so we have 6,000 Americans who were ripped off by the Cubans in the past and now the U.S. taxpayer is supposed to make unsecured loans to the same government that ripped off 6,000 others. Gee, fool me once, shame on me. Fool me twice, you know.

Mr. FEINBERG. So if that's a question, so over the last 55 years of embargo we have not succeeded in getting compensation for those Americans who did lose their properties.

So I would say under the current policy of engagement we have a better chance at least of getting some compensation for those lost properties and the Cuban Government has agreed and already we had a first round of discussions with the Cuban Government on the resolution of these claims.

As you may know, the Cuban constitution——

Mr. SHERMAN. If I could just interrupt. If we—as I understand it we allow agri-food exports to Cuba and so the question is not whether we'll have free trade in agricultural products to Cuba but whether we'll have taxpayer-subsidized——

Mr. POE. Your time has expired.

The Chair recognizes the chairman of the full committee.

Chairman ROYCE. I'm just going to be very brief because of the vote. But I'd like to submit for the record some questions.

The Obama administration has announced several regulatory changes that have allowed them to chip away at the embargo. Most recently the administration announced a regulatory loophole that will allow us to facilitate Cuba's use of U.S. dollars to make international financial transactions.

How is Cuba's banking system set up and is it sufficiently transparent is the first question I put for the record. Will the Cuban people be able to partake in such transactions or would it be for state entities only?

Would allowing such transactions be consistent with legislation passed by the U.S. Congress? In other words, would it be legal? And with current OFAC Cuba sanctions regulations that restrict Cuba's ability to transact in U.S. currency? And what have been the practical effects for the average Cuban citizen of the relaxing of OFAC Cuba sanctions regulations?

Have U.S. negotiators secured the right of Cuban workers to collect their earned wages or does the Cuban Government continue to collect wages directly from the employer to then distribute as low as 5 percent of those wages to the corresponding worker, keeping the rest for the Cuban Government?

Those are the questions I'd like to ask not only for the panel to respond to but I intend to submit that in writing to the administration as well.

Thank you, Mr. Chairman. I yield back. Thank you, Ranking Member, as well.

Mr. POE. I thank the gentleman. What the chairman was saying was he's asked you those questions so now respond in writing, if you would.

There were other questions Mr. Perry asked and there were some other members that asked questions as well. You will receive those questions again and respond within 10 days in writing to those questions.

Thank you, gentlemen, for being here today. This has been a very thought-provoking hearing. I appreciate all of your testimony and as mentioned earlier your testimony is a part of the record.

The subcommittee is adjourned.

[Whereupon, at 3:45 p.m., the committee was adjourned.]

APPENDIX

MATERIAL SUBMITTED FOR THE RECORD

SUBCOMMITTEE HEARING NOTICE
COMMITTEE ON FOREIGN AFFAIRS
U.S. HOUSE OF REPRESENTATIVES
WASHINGTON, DC 20515-6128

Subcommittee on Terrorism, Nonproliferation, and Trade
Ted Poe (R- TX), Chairman

TO: MEMBERS OF THE COMMITTEE ON FOREIGN AFFAIRS

You are respectfully requested to attend an OPEN hearing of the Committee on Foreign Affairs, to be held by the Subcommittee on Terrorism, Nonproliferation, and Trade in Room 1334 of the Longworth House Office Building (and available live on the Committee website at http://www.ForeignAffairs.house.gov):

DATE: Tuesday, March 15, 2016

TIME: 1:30 p.m.

SUBJECT: Trade with Cuba: Growth and Opportunities

WITNESSES: C. Parr Rosson, Ph.D.
                   Head of Department
                   Agricultural Economics
                   Texas A&M University

                   Mr. Ray Stoesser
                   President
                   Texas Rice Council

                   Mr. Jason Marczak
                   Director
                   Latin American Growth Initiative
                   Atlantic Council

                   Mr. Mauricio Claver-Carone
                   Executive Director
                   Cuba Democracy Advocates

                   Richard E. Feinberg, Ph.D.
                   Professor
                   School of Global Policy and Strategy
                   University of California, San Diego

By Direction of the Chairman

The Committee on Foreign Affairs seeks to make its facilities accessible to persons with disabilities. If you are in need of special accommodations, please call 202/225-5021 at least four business days in advance of the event, whenever practicable. Questions with regard to special accommodations in general (including availability of Committee materials in alternative formats and assistive listening devices) may be directed to the Committee.

COMMITTEE ON FOREIGN AFFAIRS

MINUTES OF SUBCOMMITTEE ON _____ *Terrorism, Nonproliferation, and Trade* _____ HEARING

Day____*Tuesday*____Date____*March 15, 2016*____Room_____*1334*_____

Starting Time ____*2:24 p.m.*____ Ending Time ____*3:46 p.m.*____

Recesses [____] (____to____) (____to____) (____to____) (____to____) (____to____) (____to____)

Presiding Member(s)

Chairman Ted Poe

Check all of the following that apply:

Open Session ☑
Executive (closed) Session ☐
Televised ☑

Electronically Recorded (taped) ☑
Stenographic Record ☑

TITLE OF HEARING:

"Trade with Cuba: Growth and Opportunities"

SUBCOMMITTEE MEMBERS PRESENT:

Reps. Poe, Perry, Zeldin, Keating, Sherman, Kelly

NON-SUBCOMMITTEE MEMBERS PRESENT: *(Mark with an * if they are not members of full committee.)*

Reps. Royce, Emmer*, Crawford*, Bass*

HEARING WITNESSES: Same as meeting notice attached? Yes ☑ No ☐
(If "no", please list below and include title, agency, department, or organization.)

STATEMENTS FOR THE RECORD: *(List any statements submitted for the record.)*

QFR: submitted by Rep. Ed Royce to Mr. Mauricio Claver-Carone

---

TIME SCHEDULED TO RECONVENE _____
or
TIME ADJOURNED ____*3:46 p.m.*____

Subcommittee Staff Director

Questions for the Record – Submitted by Rep. Royce

For: Mauricio Claver-Carone

Q. The Obama Administration has announced several regulatory changes that have allowed them to chip away at the embargo. Most recently, the Administration announced a regulatory loophole that will allow us to facilitate Cuba's use of U.S. dollars to make international financial transactions. How is Cuba's banking system set up and is it sufficiently transparent? Will the Cuban people be able to partake in such transactions, or would it be for state entities only? Would allowing such transactions be consistent with legislation passed by the U.S. Congress and current OFAC Cuba sanctions regulations that restrict Cuba's ability to transact in US currency?

A: The Obama Administration's efforts to promote financial ties with Cuba's shadowy, state-owned banks pose an inherent risk to the U.S.'s banking system. Most of this risk stems from the obscure, arbitrary and secretive nature of Cuba's banking system. The Cuban people remain strictly prohibited from partaking in foreign banking transactions. It remains under the exclusive purview of the Castro regime.

In *The Daily Business Review*, Fernando Capablanca, managing director at Coral Gables-based Whitecap Consulting Group, who has been studying the possibility of U.S. financial services entering Cuba for over 20 years and created the Cuban Banking Study Group, recently explained how, "the Cuban banking system, even to someone like himself who is interested in understanding it, is an obscure hodgepodge of industrial and retail banks, joint ventures with foreign financiers, export financing agencies and currency trading houses. He said the goals of many Cuban financial institutions, and even their reason for existing, is not always clear."

In recent years, European investors have seen over $1 billion arbitrarily frozen in Cuban banks by the Castro regime. As *Reuters* reported, "the Communist-run nation froze up to $1 billion in the accounts of foreign suppliers by the start of 2009."

Other reasons for concern include the Cuban regime's nefarious activities in Venezuela; the international forced labor and trafficking practices that currently represent the Cuban regime's main source of income; the massive Medicare and insurance fraud schemes that have sent millions back to Cuba through its banking system; any trafficking in properties stolen from Americans; the 2013 incident whereby the Cuban regime was caught trafficking weapons to North Korea, which was found to be the largest violation of U.N. Security Sanctions to date; and the February 2015 incident whereby the Cuban regime was caught smuggling weapons through Colombia, which may have been intended for FARC narco-terrorists. In another recent case, it's believed that the infamous Cayman Island fraudsters, known as the "Gang of Four", may have moved $450-500 million in stolen money to Cuba.

These should all raise serious concerns regarding financial transactions in -- and thru -- Cuba, particularly the origins of such funds.

Recent regulatory changes by the Obama Administration to authorize certain financial transactions with Cuba, namely U-turn transactions, are outside the statutory authority given to the President by Congress. Allowing the Castro regime to use U.S. dollars in international transactions is wholly inconsistent with the statutory mandates of the Cuban Democracy Act of 1992 and the Cuban Liberty and Democratic Solidarity Act of 1996, as it does not promote freedom, democracy or support the Cuban people.

To be absolutely clear -- "the Cuban people" are not shuffling dollars through BNP Paribas, ING Group and HSBC Bank. Only the Castro regime and its apparatchiks are able, willing and eager to do so, which inarguably contravenes U.S. interests and statutory mandates.

Q. What have been the practical effects for the average Cuban citizen of the relaxing of OFAC Cuba sanctions regulations? Have US negotiators secured the right of Cuban workers to collect their earned wages, or does the Cuban government continue to collect wages directly from the employer to then distribute as low as 5% of those wages to the corresponding worker?

A: Purportedly, the changes in Commerce and Treasury Department regulations were geared at specifically helping Cuba's "self-employment" sector grow. Yet, the opposite has been taken place -- which was entirely predictable.

Cuba's military and intelligence services control and run the conglomerates of Cuba. The "self-employment" sector represents a very small part of the island's economy and it is important, in the debate over sanctions, to understand its nature and limits. During economic crises, the Castro regime typically authorizes a host of services that Cubans can be licensed to provide, keeping at least a portion of what they may be paid. The world's news media refers to these jobs as "private enterprise," which implies "private ownership." Yet Cuba's "self-employed" licensees have no ownership rights whatsoever - be it to their artistic or "intellectual" outputs, commodity they produce, or personal service they offer. Licensees have no legal entity (hence business) to transfer, sell or leverage. They don't even own the equipment essential to their self-employment. More to the point, licensees have no right to engage in foreign trade, seek or receive foreign investments. Effectually licensees continue to work for the state -- and when the state decides such jobs are no longer needed, licensees are shut down without recourse.

Self-employment was a temporary reaction to loss of Soviet subsidies, and with the remnants of the Chavez regime in Venezuela now imploding, Cuba will likely continue allowing it. Yet the historic lesson is clear: The Castro regime only responds when it is economically pressed. Once the Cuban economy stabilizes or begins to "bounce back," the Castro government reverses itself to freeze or revoke self-employment licenses. Lift U.S. sanctions and Cuba's government will solely focus on strengthening its state conglomerates and the repression required to suppress change.

The fact remains that the Castro regime has never made any changes out of good-will, but only when forced out of necessity. Nothing has changed.

Thus, rather than empowering Cuba's "self-employed" sector, the opposite has been the case. The Castro regime's military conglomerates, led by GAESA, have been at the center of all trade delegations. Even the limited spaces in which the "self-employed" previously operated are being constricted so that GAESA can further centralize its control of the island's travel, retail and financial sector. This has led to the widespread expulsion, arrest and confiscation of the "self-employed" from designated tourist zones.

Meanwhile, a follow-up theory of the Obama Administration was that U.S. businesses would pressure Castro into allowing greater space for the "self-employment" sector to operate. Again, the exact opposite is happening.

Rather than pressuring the Castro regime, the business community is instead lobbying the Obama Administration to circumvent U.S. law and allow it to cut deals with Cuba's military monopolies.

To this day, all foreign investment in Cuba must be done through minority joint ventures with Castro's military monopolies. Moreover, all workers in Cuba must be hired through the Castro regime's state-employment agency (Grupo Palco, S.A.), which in turn, pockets upwards of 92% of those workers' salaries. These deals violate a myriad of international labor covenants, including:

• Freedom of Association and Protection to Organize Convention (No. 87) - Article 1(g) of Cuba's Labor Code grants workers "the right to associate themselves voluntarily and establish Unions." In practice, it is not allowed.

• Protection of Wages Convention (No. 05) - Cuba violates this Convention that prohibits deductions from wages with a view to insuring a direct or indirect payment for obtaining or retaining employment made to a state intermediary agency.

• Right to Organize and Collective Bargaining Convention (No. 98) - Collective bargaining is non-existent in Cuba.

• Discrimination (Employment and Occupation) Convention (No. 111) - By the Castro regime selecting the workers to supply to foreign investors, Cuba does not follow the mandate of equality of opportunity or treatment in employment and occupation.

• Employment Policy Convention (No. 122) - Cuba's policy of selecting who works where, regardless of skills or endowments, and transfers are not the result of the will of the worker.

• The Universal Declaration of Human Rights (Article 23) - Nonexistent in Cuba are: the right to work; free choice of employment; just and favorable working conditions; protection against unemployment; the right to equal pay for equal work; just and favorable remuneration; and the right to form and join trade unions.

The biggest losers -- the Cuban people.